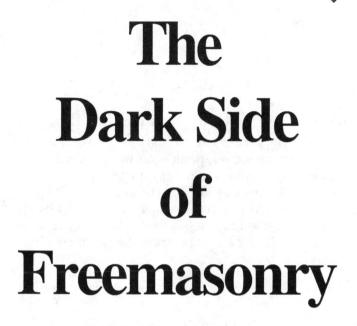

The Dark Side of Freemasonry

edited by
J. Edward Decker

Huntington House Publishers

Huntington House Publishers
P.O. Box 53788
Lafayette, Louisiana 70505

Library of Congress Card Catalog Number 94-77033
ISBN 1-56384-061-8

Contents

Introduction

In June of 1993, I had the pleasure of speaking at a national conference for the leaders of ministries to Masons. It was held in Knoxville, Tennessee and was attended by people who were involved in ministering to those in and around the many Masonic fraternities. Also, there were many of those who write and speak on the subject, as well as some of the leading researchers on the subject. It was a great place to be if you were interested in the subject and probably the worst place to be if you were the subject of the interest.

Seldom before in my career as an apologist for the Christian faith had I come across a more zealous crowd of evangelical believers. I was rather fortunate to be one of the very first speakers, which meant that I could sit back after I finished, relax, and listen to the rest of the presentations, even sleep through a few if I felt like it. It was a rare "out of gear" time for me.

My relaxation was short-lived, however. The very next speaker brought me to rapt attention, and I spent the rest of the trip on the edge of my chair soaking in some of the best instruction on the subject of Freemasonry that I had ever witnessed.

As excited as I was to be receiving such great information, I was morose over the fact that there should have been thousands in attendance instead of hundreds. It was

as though something dramatic needed to be done to
capture the moment, to save the data in order to bring it
to the church at large, the church that has let this secret
cancer into its sanctuaries and eat away at its underside.

I was determined not to let this information be buried away in obscurity the day after the conference closed.
I went to a number of those who presented papers there
and asked their permission to publish their material in a
book. Obviously, they agreed, and you are reading the
introduction to that compilation.

This is a great book. It contains the bulk of the Christian stand on just about every aspect of Freemasonry and
the lodges. I have tried to get it all in order, tying it
together in a readable and usable fashion.

There will be times when you will read the same
charges, the same references and the same Scriptures
from chapter to chapter. I have left them in to give you
the perspective of each author on their subject of interest. We have dissected the dangerous doctrines of Masonry, and there is nothing left but the ashes of a false
system of darkness.

I pray, on behalf of each man and woman who has
contributed to this work, that it be a blessing to those
who study it with the purpose of using its information for
the salvation of lost souls and for the edification of the
body of Christ toward that goal of becoming the
unblemished bride of Christ.

Every person who has contributed to this work has as
first priority the ministry of grace to the lost. They are
not the enemies of those in Masonry, but their friends.
Each is willing to correspond and minister on an individual basis and can be reached through the offices of
Huntington House Publishers.

One

Freemasonry and the Church: A Christian Worker's Perspective

J. Edward Decker

I have never been a Mason although I grew up in a Masonic family and was a member of its youth organization, the DeMolay. Every male member of my family since 1805 has been active in the Masonic lodge. My dad was a Mason until he repented of it two years before he passed away in 1992. My mother was an Eastern Star and my grandfather was a Thirty-third Degree Mason. All my uncles, aunts, and grandparents and the people on every side of my family have been involved in Masonry, not only here in the United States but in Europe before we came to the United States.

Those of you who know my background know that I spent twenty years of my life in Mormonism. I became a Christian in 1975, and since that time I have been ministering the gospel of grace to the Mormon people. What does this all have to do with the subject of the lodge and Freemasonry? Prior to my time as a Mormon, I was a member of the Episcopal church, and almost everybody in our local parish was a Mason. It was a Masonic organization in a lot of ways, although I didn't think much of it at the time.

There came a point in my life when I felt the urge to go out and seek some undefined "religious truth." It was unique that the church I ran into immediately was the Mormon church. I often wondered why that was the case. Why didn't I run into a Baptist or another Episcopalian who wasn't bored to death in the high church with all its rituals. Why did I suddenly find the Mormons?

We are dealing in areas of spiritual power in some of these things, and I believe that the same spirit that was in that local Episcopal church (because of the immense power that the Masons had in it) was the same controlling spirit that is in Mormonism because Mormonism is permeated throughout with Masonic doctrines.

Joseph Smith was a Mason. His brother Hiram was a Mason. The first five presidents of the Mormon church were Masons. The Mormon Masonic lodge in Nauvoo, Illinois, was one of the largest Masonic lodges in the United States at the time. They had over fourteen hundred members in one lodge. So much of what I did in Mormonism had very close ties into Masonry.

I remember being in a Baptist church a few years after I became a Christian. I was sharing some of the things I had done in Mormonism and I talked about my participation in the Mormon temple ritual. I shared some things about the temple like the oaths that we took, the symbolism, some of the signs and tokens, and the apron that Lucifer, who is the instructor in part of the Mormon temple ritual, wore.

I told them that the apron he wore had Masonic symbols on it, and several of these same symbols were on the veil at the end of the Mormon temple ritual. We Mormons extended our arms through these holes in the veil and put our arms around God, or the man playing the part of God. At the veil, we recited all these "special" things that we learned in the temple. Those holes were really the Masonic square, rule, and compass slit in the veil. We also wore those same marks on our sacred undergarments which we Mormons must wear as Temple Mormons.

(It's interesting to note that since we began revealing these secrets to the world, the LDS god has given new instructions or revelation word to his prophets in Salt Lake City, and many of these Masonic blood oaths have been removed from the ritual.)

At the end of that meeting in the Baptist church, I walked to the back of the church to say good-bye to people. An elder, a member of the board from that church, came up and led me off to a corner of the back area of the church where, with great stress in his voice, he said, "You better stop doing this."

I responded, "Stop doing what?"

He said, "You better stop talking about those things."

"Talking about what things?"

"You better stop talking about those rituals because you are sharing secrets that only Masons are supposed to know."

I said, "I beg your pardon. I don't know what you're talking about."

"No, you know exactly what I'm talking about. You stop it! When you're talking about the Mormon temple ritual, you're revealing the Masonic ritual secrets. You know that the thumb to the throat oath and all the things that are done in the Mormon temple are things that are Masonic secrets. Those hand shakes, the signs, the tokens, the handclasps, the penalties, and all these things are Masonic, and you're revealing the Masonic stuff."

"I'm not revealing Masonic stuff; I'm revealing what I did, what I personally did in the Mormon temple," I replied with some force.

"You stop it or you're going to get hurt. You don't know what you are doing. You don't know what troubles you're heading for if you don't stop this!"

I said, "I'm not stopping it. I think its abominable and Luciferian, and I'm going to talk about it because I think people need to know what is going on in the Mormon temple."

Finally he just said, "Well if you're saying that the Mormons do that, and it's Satanic, what are you saying about Masonry?"

Not knowing much except what little I could get out of the Bible, I just said, "If Masonry is involved with the same rituals and the same blood oaths, it's from the same pit of Hell." The elder turned away in anger and stomped off. I stood there, watching after him and then I saw that the pastor had been standing over to the side and had watched the entire exchange. He looked at me and slowly shook his head. He said, "You're being a very foolish young man. You don't know what you're doing; you don't know what troubles you are headed for if you don't stop this." He turned quickly and walked out of the church. I stood there thinking, "Hey, I'm in a Christian church, and the Christians are getting mad at me and threatening me. What am I doing wrong? I'm talking about evil that I participated in, and suddenly I'm having problems." I thought, "This is it, I'm going to find out about Masonry. I have to know what's going on here."

About a month after that, my friend's dad passed away, and my wife and I were sitting in their church attending his funeral in a very nice evangelical situation. The family was sitting there in the front row with friends gathered around them. We finally reached the end of the funeral, and, as the pastor was thanking us for attending, suddenly the hair stood up on the back of my neck.

I turned and looked toward the back of the church and saw this group of men marching down the aisle in these black somber outfits and carrying scrolls, and all kinds of things, wearing white gloves, boxer-type hats, aprons with all kinds of Masonic markings on them. They marched up to the front and gathered around the coffin.

They began chanting and breaking leaves over the coffin and so forth. I broke out into spiritual hysteria. I began praying quietly to myself; I was almost on my knees, and my wife was praying just as hard beside me. We were trying to bind this evil that had just come into this place. We didn't know what it was that was happening, we just knew it was bad. Of course, it was a Masonic funeral ritual.

I talked to my dad about it since he was still a Mason at the time. I said something about the Masonic funeral being horrible. He said, "What do you mean horrible? I'm going to be buried in a Masonic funeral myself."

I said, "Not if I have anything to say about it."

He said, "I'm going to be cremated in my white apron, my lambskin apron, and I want the Masons to do it."

I said, "I can't do that, Dad. It is a dark, pagan thing, and it is not the way a Christian needs to leave this world."

Dad had his will rewritten and had papers drawn up so that my non-Christian sister would be the executrix of his estate. He did that so I could not get near his body after he died, so he could be cremated in his lambskin apron.

(Jumping ahead in my story a bit, I need to share with you that Dad repented of Freemasonry two years before his homegoing. He had been a Mason for over sixty years, but Jesus set him free. We had a believer's memorial service for my dad, a time of joy and peaceful release. Isn't God faithful!)

So, I began an intense study. I'm extremely well versed in it now. I have probably close to a thousand books on Masonry in my library. Most of them are esoteric books that are written by Masons. Some of them actually say, "Esoteric Book, Do Not Let Non-Masons Read."

I have been able, through the grace of God, to get into some places in which I don't belong. I have acquired all the ritual books for all the rituals of Masonry in their associated groups, from the Eastern Star to Job's Daughters to Rainbow Girls, to all the various groups. I have

every ritual of every step of Freemasonry in the York Rite
and the Scottish Rite, Blue Lodge, Shriner, and Red Man
and Jesters, and all the esoteric groups in Masonry. I have
just about every document that they ever dared to put in
writing, plus I have the testimony of thousands of Masons
who have been set free from that darkness. So, I can talk
a little bit about Masonry.

Masonry is one of the most volatile subjects in the
Christian church today. Where did Masonry come from?
The Mason will tell you that it started back in Solomon's
Temple and that, ritually, it carried on and continued
through the building of the great cathedrals of Europe.
Their history is the history of the stone masons; they were
called the operative masons.

Because they didn't have plastic badges in those days,
they learned secret hand shakes and signs so that a master mason could go from cathedral to cathedral, from
country to country and go to the boss man there and give
him a secret hand shake or secret sign. By that sign, the
construction boss would know that he was a master mason, or an apprentice mason or journeyman mason. It
was pretty simple, but it worked for them. The special
sign or handshake would identify the worker in different
levels of capability. Because of the importance of keeping
the craft free from impostors, there were some serious
penalties for lying or using a code you hadn't earned.

That's where Freemasonry really came from. In the
late seventeenth century or early eighteenth century, they
began to gather in the towns and cities in fellowship off
the jobs. They allowed noncraftsmen friends, called non-
operative masons to join with them socially. That is when
Freemasonry as we see it today, or Speculative Masonry,
began. Now, that's their story. And, for the most part,
that's pretty much what most of what I'll call "social Masonry" still is today. However, that's not what "spiritual,"
or "mystical," Masonry is really all about.

Spiritual/mystical Masonry actually goes back, not to
the temple of Solomon, but to the Crusades when Eastern Mysticism was brought into the Church through the

Knights Templar. The Crusaders brought back esoteric ritual into central Europe, France, and Italy. They brought back the Kabalah and Eastern Mysticism, and they brought in the Egyptian and the Gnostic mysteries that were present, even in the days of Christ.

They conformed these findings into sixteenth and seventeenth century terminology and wove them into the culture of Europe in those days. Even first century Christianity had the Essenes, who brought a Gnostic superiority into the fringe of the Church. They claimed secret knowledge that only the adept were allowed to receive. They were also known as the apron-wearers.

It's interesting that they wore aprons, which were their protection, their covering before God. The Essenes wore these same aprons that the Masons wear today. And, if you go back to the Babylonian mysteries and the deification of Nimrod, the priests of Nimrod also wore those same aprons in his temple. And, they too were known as the apron-wearers. They also wore special undergarments with special markings on the breasts, just like the Mormons do today.

There's nothing new under the sun. And, old Satan is still whining the same old record over and over again with different names, the same things you see today in the new age; it's the same things the Essenes and the early Masons embraced: higher knowledge, becoming one with universe, becoming one with the essence of the Christ spirit. All these things tie into modern Masonry.

The power base of early Masonry was tied to the tremendous wealth and power of the Knights Templar, until the Roman Catholic church, attempting to break the power grip of the craft, outlawed them and began to confiscate its land and treasure houses, killing its leaders when and where they could. The Masons, particularly through a group called the Illuminati, had great power on the political scene. We see a Masonic hand in the French Revolution and the American Revolution. There is a thread, a theme here that demonstrates the Masons have surely had a conspiratorial part of modern, international history.

How could that happen on such a scale over so many years? It could happen right here on a small scale. Suppose everybody in this group swore solemn oaths to join together as a secret band. Suppose we closed the door, we locked the room, and we brought each of you up and had you kneel down, kiss a Bible, and swear a blood oath to have your throat slit from ear to ear if you broke your oath. And, suppose you swore an oath that you would do everything in your power for the rest of your life for the people who are in this select group, right here in this room. That's no one else, but just those of us who are in this select group. We would do beneficial things for each other. If someone had an opening in their company and you needed a job, they would move you to that job over someone else. Or, if there was a contract being led by my company, I would see that you got the contract. And, we would begin to take advantage of the political and the economic system to better each of us. We would have a good thing going. Right? Almost like a secret fraternity.

That's what the Skull and Bones Society is that former president Bush belongs to out of Yale. That's exactly what they did. They swore these blood oaths that they would help each other in the political and the economic society, to lift each other up, to support them in everything that they did. They swore blood oaths to do this. It has been pretty effective for most of them. And, if you look at the simple side of Masonry, basically that's what began to take place.

In 1717, in England, the first Grand Lodge met. So, we know that there were many lodges for a Grand Lodge to meet and be organized under the Grand Lodge of England. In the United States, many of the people who were involved in the implementation of the Revolutionary War and the first Congress were Masons. The Declaration of Independence was written on a Masonic white lambskin apron. If you go over to Washington, D.C., today and look at this great document, you will find it written on a lambskin apron.

That's interesting because my dad wanted to be buried in it because it was his covering before God, until

Jesus became his covering. Only a pagan needs to find some cover before God.

If you are a pagan, there is no problem being a Mason because it's a pagan society. If you are a Christian, you have a problem. Let me explain the problem. It's almost a simple matter of submission to the spirit of darkness. When a man goes into the Masonic order, before he can even enter, he has to be voted on by the lodge. They use a secret voting system using white balls and black balls, and, if anybody puts just one black ball in the box (that's where the expression being black-balled comes from), you cannot ever be a Mason. If any man decides he doesn't like the color of your hair, if you have offended him in business, if there is some offense in your relationship, he can then just put a black ball in, no questions asked, and you are not a member of the lodge.

When a man goes into the first, or Entered Apprentice, level, he is given slippers, he takes most of his regular clothes off, he has one pants leg off, he has his chest bare, his wedding ring removed, he has a hood or blindfold put over him, he has a rope tied around his neck (called a cabletow), and he's led around that way through most of the ritual. He is a man in darkness seeking the light of the lodge.

I wonder how many of these men would do this if their wives or children were watching. If there's anything that I do that I can't do with my wife or I can't do with my son or my daughters, then I'm in trouble; I don't care what it is. There's nothing in my life that I would do that I had to hide from my wife. So, if I'm going to go in and share a secret oath that I can never reveal to my wife, I'm in deep trouble.

First, I couldn't do it because I would never do something that I would have to hide from my own wife because she's one with me in Christ. So, at the start, I've got a problem. Secondly, as a Christian, I don't need the light of the lodge because I already have the light of Jesus Christ. And, so I'm not in darkness seeking the light of the lodge or the light of the knowledge of man. They could put sixteen hoods over my head, and I'm still in light because I'm in Christ. But, if I allow myself to be submitted to that, and I kneel down and swear a blood oath to keep the secrets that I'm learning and that I will hide the sins of my fellow Masons, murder and treason excepted, I am no longer in fellowship with Christ. As a Christian, I cannot swear that oath. These are simple things here. Thirdly is the Masonic relationship with Jesus.

I spoke to a Mason a short time ago. He is in the Blue Lodge, which is the lower level encompassing the first three levels of Masonry, so he's really in the lower level. He told me he was a Christian. I said, "Do you love the Lord Jesus Christ?"

He answered, "Yes, of course I do. There is nothing in Masonry that would offend Jesus Christ."

I said, "Are you sure there is nothing that you do in Masonry that would be offensive to Jesus?"

He said, "Ed, nothing that I do in the Blue Lodge would ever offend the Lord Jesus Christ."

"Do you love the Lord?" I asked.

"Of course I do!"

"Do you believe the Word of God?"

"Yes, of course I do!"

"Do you live the Word of God?"

"Yes, well, at least I do my best!"

"Well, then, if you love the Lord Jesus Christ, then you'll do what he says, and you will not do what he says not to do. So, how can you be a Mason?"

"What are you talking about?"

I said, "Well, Jesus himself says to swear no oath. Let your yes be yes and your no, no. He said anything more comes of evil."

He looked at me for a long minute and finally responded, "Yeah, but that's, you know, symbolic."

I said, "I'm sorry, but it's not symbolic. It's the Word of God."

That's the simplest, most direct answer to the lodges. As Christians, we are not to swear any oath. So, we don't swear oaths. We must let our yes be yes and our no, no.

In the very beginning of their ritual journey, when the Masons receive that white apron, which my dad treasured so greatly, they are told how wonderful it will be to see God, and then the fruit of all men's lives shall be made known. They are told in the "apron lecture" that their apron shall be their covering when they stand before the great white throne judgment of God. And, yet, they just slide right through that ritual.

The great white throne judgment of God is the judgment of the damned. The twentieth chapter of Revelation, says that those who are not in Christ will be raised up to go to the great white throne judgment of God; Christ is the only acceptable covering for sin. However, the Masons are not the first to try to use other means. This lie is found all the way back in the third chapter of Genesis when man first tried to cover his sin with an apron of his own making. God rejected it then, and He still rejects it today; whether it's the Masons or the Mormons, God is not pleased.

Lucifer, himself, tells the Mormons to wear the apron in the Mormon temple ritual. He says, "Look, here comes Father; quick, cover yourselves." And, they cover themselves. In that ritual, Lucifer is actually wearing an apron that resembles that of a Past Worshipful Master. Sitting back behind all this, Satan has to laugh at our stupidity.

One of the men at the conference told me that he was the Past Worshipful Master of a lodge, and he recalled with me the ceremony that the Masons perform in which the initiate goes through a mock death and resurrection. He is raised up from death by the power of the Strong Grip, the Lion's Paw Grip, by the power of the Master of the lodge, who is supposed to have that position of resurrection power to raise him from the dead. He becomes born again, symbolically in Masonry, by the power of the

Strong Grip, or the Lion's Paw Grip, which is the secret or sacred grip of the Master in the Blue Lodge. But, to the Christian, Jesus is the resurrection of life and not the Master of any lodge, not the power of the Strong Grip and not the power of the Masonic Order.

The Blue Lodge Masons, encompassing the first three degrees of Masonry, are instructed that they are seeking the lost word, or the lost name of God. The rituals are built around this idea; they're seeking greater knowledge. Yet, some of the leading Masons and in some of the rituals of the higher levels, they smile condescendingly at the Blue Lodge.

At the higher levels, they teach that the Blue Lodge is just the outer courtyard of true Masonry and that those who are involved in the Blue Lodge are led to believe that they are getting answers but they are being misled, even when they think they are being led properly. They are not allowed to know the truth because the truth is only for those who prove their worthiness. Sounds like Mormonism again. Only at the higher levels can they get the real knowledge, but the Blue Lodge is purposely misled with allegory and misleading symbolism. They think they are gaining knowledge, but these people are actually being fooled by the higher levels of Gnostic Masons. It isn't until they reach the level of Royal Arch Masonry that they discover that the lost name of God wasn't lost after all. It's at this level that they learn the sacred name of God.

They find that the sacred name of God is composed of three names representing the three identities of God. It is so sacred that it takes three Royal Arch Masons to be able to speak it. One Mason cannot say the full name of God, which is Jaobulon. The three Masons grip hands high and low and chant, "Jao-bul-on, Jao-bul-on, Jao-bul-on, Je-hov-ah." The Masonic material identifies the three as Jehovah, Baal, and Osiris.

What these men are doing is worshipping a demon god so far removed from the real God that this worship must surely defile the holiness of God and guarantee those who pronounce that name in such a ceremony a

stand among the thousands of graves where so many Americans were buried. I was going through all the names of the American servicemen who died, and I noticed that everybody who had won a congressional medal of honor had an inverted five-pointed star next to his name. And, there were three little dots at the end of each star point, which are Masonic dots; you'll see them in all the Masonic material. I wondered why it was on there, so I did a little research and discovered that it actually is the design of the United States Congressional Medal of Honor. It's a pentagram, a literal pentagram.

The inverted five-pointed star in a circle is one of the most powerful Satanic emblems in the universe as far as Satanists are concerned. That's the Congressional Medal of Honor! As I researched that, I discovered that it was designed by Masons. I also discovered that the Statue of Liberty was a gift of the Masonic brethren in France to the American Masons, and it too is filled with Masonic, occult symbols all over it.

I discovered in Washington, D.C., that the streets around the White House were laid out by a Masonic architect, and they are laid out in the form of the Goat of Mendes and the square and compass of Freemasonry. The Capitol building and its streets actually form the Goat of Mendes, and the square and the compass of Freemasonry intersect the Washington Monument right in dead line with it. The left leg of the Masonic compass sits on top of the White House, and the right leg sits on the Jefferson Memorial. Jefferson was a Deist and a Mason and an Illuminati member. So was Benjamin Franklin.

These great men, who are highly esteemed for their great work in establishing our country, were also busy laying in the root of occult power, a conspiracy designed to mystically affect our nation's capital. Designed in the streets themselves, and with its southern point sitting in the center of the White House, is an inverted five-pointed star which again is the geometric face of the Goat of Mendes. And, you wonder why we have stargazers in the White House.

The other thing that bothered me while I was re-
searching this in Washington, D.C., was the fact that every federal building that exists has been prayed for and
set apart by the Masons in their ritual. They have the
cornerstones filled with their own paraphernalia, their
own prayers to Jaobulon. It's only because God still has
prayer-power Christians in this nation that we haven't
succumbed to these things.

But, these are the things of darkness that we must
fight against today. We have a door opened to Satan's
kingdom sitting right in our national capital. There is a
dark spiritual power that sits over our country today
because of this. I believe that we need to stand up against
it spiritually.

In the ritual of the Blue Lodge, Masons are sworn to
keep the secrets of their brethren, murder and treason
excepted. In the Royal Arch degree, the one where they
learn the name of their god, they swear that same oath,
murder and treason included. What chance does a non-
Mason have going into a court of law against Masons
when there is a Masonic judge and Masonic attorneys. All
a Mason has to do is let a Masonic judge, or even a
Masonic juror, know that he is a Masonic brother, and
that is that.

Sometimes you look at the way a case is going, and it
just doesn't make sense. We had one in Seattle not too
long ago; in fact, the union my sister worked for was
involved in it, and nothing went right, even simple points
that were obvious to everyone but the judge. They couldn't
figure out what was wrong, so I asked her, "Are the
defendants and the judge Masons?" She checked it out
and found out that they were. I said,

> You don't have a chance. There is no way you can
> win because they passed the word to the judge in
> the lodge or they gave that judge a signal; they
> gave him the sign of the square, or the sign of
> distress, gave him one of a dozen different signs
> they could give him, and that judge was bound by
> his Masonic code to find for his brother. He is

going to do that for the Mason whether he's right
or wrong.

In another case a few years ago, a wealthy business-
man was accused of molesting his granddaughter. I knew
that he was a Mason held in high esteem in the city. I was
surprised to see that the judge in his case was a well-
known Shriner and wondered how the judge was going to
act for the state in the matter and also uphold his Masonic oaths.

A week into the highly publicized case, the judge
came in one morning and announced that he had made
a grave error in allowing certain testimony. He said the
error was quite grave since it meant that he had to dis-
miss the charges. He said his error would not allow the
man to get a fair trial ever and, therefore, he could not
be recharged. The judge took an official reprimand and,
yet, sits on the bench today a Mason of high honor. What
Christian living as a disciple of Christ could sit by and see
that take place and, yet, remain in the lodge?

Masons can't even talk about Jesus as Lord and Savior
in the Masonic Lodge because Jesus is recognized as a
great teacher only and not the Word that became Flesh.
He is merely one of the great teachers, the same as Buddha, the first legislator in Masonry. And, Jesus, Moses,
Zoroaster, and Socrates are all parts or pieces of one
great truth. The Masons say that they do not look at the
individual, they look at the truth that they bring. The only
requirement is to believe in a supreme being, and, therefore, people who are in Islam can be involved in it. They
worship a stone idol sitting in the Kaaba and believe that
is really God. They can actually be Masons because they
believe in their own deity. And Jesus isn't being represented there in a form that should be acceptable to any
Christian.

In the Masonic lodge, the Holy Scriptures take the
same devaluation even though they have a Bible there.
Yet, when they quote the Scripture in the ritual, if it were
compared word for word to the Bible, you would find
that the name of Jesus has been taken out. It sure sounds
good, but Jesus is washed away.

In the thirtieth level of the Scottish Rite, the Masons take the communion of the dead. As they take their communion, they drink the wine out of the top of a human skull and are told that they have taken in the blood of those great teachers. In the same ritual, when they eat the bread, they are told they have eaten the bodies of those great bearers of light. It is an abomination for a Christian to partake in this occult type of the Roman Catholic ritual of transubstantiation, partaking in the literal blood and flesh of Christ, which in itself is a nonbiblical rite.

When the Masons make it to the thirty-second degree, they can decide to go into the shrine, and this is where a whole new set of problems come into sight. I have often heard a Shriner say, "There is nothing that I do in the Shrine that I wouldn't be pleased to be involved in with my family." But, when I mention a few things in the ritual and initiation, they change the subject very quickly because some of it is obscene. I know that I would never want my wife to see me doing some of those things. But, that's the superficial problem.

The really obscene thing is that at the end of that demeaning initiation, they kneel down at an altar, and they pray and swear a blood oath that is four and a half pages long including penalties that say if you reveal the secrets, you'll have your eyeballs pierced with a three-edged blade and other fun stuff. At the end of this oath, which in advance they agree is nonrevocable, they say, "And may Allah, the god of Arab, Moslem and Mohammedan, the God of our fathers, support me to the entire fulfillment of the same, Amen, Amen, Amen."[1] What a pitfall for the Shriner who claims to be a Christian! Allah is not another name for God. Allah is a tribal deity, a stone or wooden idol carved by the hand of man, and it sits entombed in the sacred black building, the Kaaba, in Mecca, where all of Islam bows down to it. Allah is a demon god who has destroyed nation after nation of followers. And, the Shriners who submit themselves to the godship of Allah have submitted themselves to demonic headship.

It bothers me every time I see the Shriners marching in a parade. They are usually busy with their little cars or motorcycles, zipping around with their red fezzes. I did a little study on the red fez. The fez comes from the name of the city of Fez, a city in Morocco, in North West Africa. In the early eighth century, the city was overrun by Islamic hordes. They came into the Christian city of Fez and demanded that they convert to Islam or be slaughtered. They refused. The Muslims took every man, woman, and child, brought them into the square, and butchered them and cut their bodies apart. These were true Christian martyrs who died for Christ: forty-five thousand men, women, and children. The Muslim butchers took their white hats and dipped them in the blood of the dying Christian children and women and wore it as a symbol of their honor.

When a man says that he is a Christian and comes into a Christian church after having just left a lodge or parade where he wore that red fez, God must cry out in agony over that wickedness. It's an abomination to God. How can a man wear a hat on his head that symbolizes by its color, by its very name, the butchering of Christian martyrs and call himself a Christian. I wouldn't want to be within seventeen light-years of him when he sees the Lord Jesus Christ when He comes because I can tell you what's going to happen to him. God will exert the penalty of the deaths of every one of those martyrs, and all the children's burn hospitals of the world will not make up for it.

Several years ago, a daily newspaper in Florida, the *Orlando Sentinel,* published a report on the Shrine hospital program. Ninety-eight percent of the money the Shriners raise in these circuses wasn't going to the hospitals; it went to the Shriners for their parties. Ninety-eight percent went to their little cars and their little boats and their temples and their little hats. Two percent went to the hospitals. Wouldn't it be wonderful if these men rejected that and put it aside and said, "I'm going to follow Christ! Christ is my Lord; Christ is my Savior, and I'm going to follow Him. I'm going to put this stuff aside even if there is a shred of a doubt."

But, let me tell you where the real sin is. If you think this is bad, I've got news for you. I'll tell you where it's really bad. After years of intense study, after having lived in this thing my entire life with my dad, my family, and my grandfather; after generation after generation in my family and seeing it in my church; and seeing it throughout churches in the United States and all over the world, I have found the deepest sin in Freemasonry. I've been all over the world with this message; I've also been run out of a few towns with it; I've also been poisoned for it, and I'm alive today and still talking!

The deepest sin of the lodge is if a Mason, as a father, as a husband, sets himself to the spiritual whoredoms I have exposed, he will reap the harvest. But, it isn't going to be in him that it will be reaped, but in his wife and his children's lives and his children's children to the third and fourth generations. He has walked away from Christ, placing Him in with Buddha and Zoroaster, and has surrendered himself to the law of the Old Testament by getting involved with these Baal worshipers. He has removed himself from godly headship, and he has opened the door to every Satanic attack in the entire world to his wife and his kids whom he says he loves.

If you have rebellion in your home; if you have whoredoms in your family and fornications, homosexuality, alcoholism, infidelity and these kinds of problems; if there is sickness and no joy and no victory in your Christian walk, it's because the door to your home has been open to Baal. The demons of hell can walk right through your front door and why? Because sitting in that lower left-hand corner of that lower drawer of your dresser is the white lambskin apron of the fraternity and all the other paraphernalia that is associated with it. You are worshipping at a false altar, and you have submitted your family to that false altar.

In the name of the Lord Jesus Christ, we have to stand up against this. We have to stand up against it in our family. If I were a Mason reading this today, I would go home, and I would burn my Masonic materials. I would get on my knees before God, I would go to my church and ask my pastor to let me go up before the congregation, confess my sin, and repent publicly because I have brought whoredoms into the congregation. This is the kind of sin that this is. The Mason has brought whoredom into the congregation. When I speak about this in churches, I say,

> Hey, you know how we do it, everybody bow their heads, everybody's eyes closed, stick up your hand and we'll pray for you. Well, not this time! No. You've brought whoredom into the congregation, you have defiled the congregation of the Holy. I want every eye up, I want every eye looking, and I want you to stand up and repent publicly in front of the whole congregation, because it is that kind of sin.

I've seen forty men in a single church stand up and repent. And, I've also seen some sit there. I was down in First Christian Church in Port Charlotte, Florida, and, at the end of the meeting, I spoke and asked the men to stand up and repent. We had a lot of men and women repent. They stood, and we prayed for them. There was a Worshipful Master present at that meeting. He was brought there by one of the deacons of the church who was a Mason, and the deacon sat there with a grimace on his face the whole time we were praying for those who stood. Then, I did what I normally do, and I said, "Those of you who have family who are involved in it, let's put a hedge about you, a spiritual hedge. Let's break the power of Masonry over your family. Let's put an end to this. We can come together in agreement to break the power over this church, to break the power over your family. For those of you who want to pray to break the power over your families, I want you to stand."

At that moment, this man's whole family, his wife and his kids, stood up right next to him, and they prayed along with all the rest. I smiled and thought, "Brother, you are in deep trouble at home." I wouldn't want to be in his shoes for anything because his wife and his kids had made a spiritual commitment to the Lord to put an end to Masonry's control of their family. God heard their cries!

At the end of that church service, the pastor stood up in his church and said, "Right now, I'm telling every Mason in this church, you have a week to either repent or get out. That's as simple as I can make it. And, if you think you have enough power in this church to vote me out in a meeting, then vote me out because I will not be a pastor of a church that has Masons in control." He took that stand, and it broke the power of Masonry over that church. I talked to that pastor several months later, and he said there was revival in the church. Friends, it was because they got rid of Baal worship in the congregation. How can the Holy Spirit of God operate in a church where the leaders, the board, and even the pastor are involved in this kind of spiritual harlotry? Our God will not share His glory with an idol!

What about the York Rite? So many contact me who say that while the many other branches of Freemasonry are certainly pagan, the York Rite is a Christian rite from start to finish. Would that it were true. First, the deep roots of Freemasonry are entwined within every branch of the craft and go through every level of paganism, cultic and occult practices right into the depths of Luciferic rituals. No part of the system is exempt. The York Rite is no different, and those men within it who claim it is free from any non-Christian influence are either blind fools or lying through their teeth!

Let's look at the Knights Templar Degree. It is reported to have originally been established to preserve and protect the craft. The special garb worn in the degree consists of an apron, sash, and cordon. The center of the apron displays a hand holding a severed head dripping blood. On the flap is a hand holding a knife. Drops of red blood cover the white background. The sash is white with a yellow fringe. It is filled with gory, severed heads, arms, and legs, mixed in with knives, crosses, and crowns. The cordon, which goes around the neck, is dark satin with severed heads down the side and a small ceremonial sword as the breast ornament. Along with these grotesque items is a human skull cut and pinned so that the top of the skull can be detached to use as a drinking vessel. And, they call this the *Christian Rite?*

The paraphernalia of this ritual should be evidence enough that the York Rite is every bit as pagan as the Scottish Rite, but let me finish this up with a few excerpts from the rite, itself. The obligation in this degree, called the Master's Nine of Elect, is now given to the candidate in the usual form. While the candidate is kneeling at the altar, the companions all stand over him with raised poniards as if about to stab him. Meanwhile, a horrible, bloody head sits on the altar facing him. He swears this blood oath:

> I do solemnly swear, in the presence of Almighty God, that I will revenge the assassination of our worthy Master, Hiram Abiff, not only on the murderers, but also on all who may betray the secrets of this degree; and furthermore, that I will keep and protect this Order with all my might, and the brethren, in general, with all my power, and furthermore, that I will obey the decrees of the Grand Council of Princes of Jerusalem; and, if I violate my obligation, I consent to be struck with the dreadful poniard of vengeance, now presented to me, and to have my head cut off, and stuck on the highest pole, or pinnacle, in the eastern part of the world, as a monument of my villainy! Amen! Amen! Amen! Amen!

The vows here are sealed with the Fifth Libation or the Sealed Obligation. The candidate is given the human skull filled with wine, which he drinks after swearing that "the sins of the person whose skull this once was, be heaped upon my head, in addition to my own; and may appear in judgment against me, both here and hereafter, should I violate or transgress any obligation in Masonry, or the Orders of [this] knighthood. . . ."

I am sorry, but any man who has sworn such oaths has so violated his Christian faith that I suspect he and all those over whom he has headship have been removed from that umbrella of Christ's protection. If your church is dying, if evangelism is a foreign word in your congregation, if there is discord within its ranks, if some small clique of people control the board and the decisions, check it out. The Baal worshippers may be in control, and the Holy Spirit of God may be going to church down the street.

Well, I've covered a lot of things that are important, and I think that we have to take a strong, godly stand on Freemasonry. If you wonder why you don't have victory in your family, now you may understand. I believe that Masonry is a multigenerational curse. I saw this in my own family until my dad was set free.

My dad had to be led through the sinner's prayer about every six months. He kept losing the witness of his salvation; he lost his joy. My dad used to run out of communion services because he feared communion in the church. He took the communion of the lodge, but he wouldn't take communion in the church. He had no joy; he had anger and hostility and bitterness.

Dad went into the hospital in early February of 1990 for emergency surgery. He had six by-passes for critical heart failure. It was so bad that they did it late at night on a weekend because they didn't think he would last until the morning. Dad was certain that because he was eighty years old and in poor health, he wasn't going to survive such an operation. He called me to his side and told me that he loved me and I was right about Masonry. Dad repented that night and prayed with me as he set things right with the Lord. Dad told my mother not to let the Masons near his body. He didn't want the apron. He wasn't going to the great white throne judgment. He was going to the banqueting table!

Well, God gave my dad a special grace. Not only did he pull through like a trooper, but he felt no pain even though he had stitches running from his neck to his toes. The morning after the operation, we had gone home for a little while and a Lutheran minister came into the room and asked my dad if there was anything he could do for him. Dad said, "Yes, please, can you give me communion?" My dad was set free in Christ. Finally, my dad's days of running away from God were over. The joy and the peace and the firm security of his salvation were there until the day he did go home to be with Jesus a little over two years later, with his family at his side singing the hymns he loved and praising God for a father, a husband, and a grandfather who had made his peace with God.

Endnotes

1. *The Ancient Arabic Order, Nobles of the Mystic Shrine* (Chicago, Ill.: Ezra A. Cook Publications, Inc., 1975), 20–22.

Two

The Public School Connection

Tom McKenney

Why are Freemasonry, the New Age, and Mormonism so determined to promote public schools while resisting Christian schools, private academies, and home schooling?

The Masonic Commitment

In my earliest studies of Freemasonry, I noticed a curious thing: one of its principal public policies is to promote and defend the public school system[1]—not just schools, but public schools. I wondered about it but decided that it must be just a public relations gimmick, something to make the Masonic lodge system look wholesome, respectable, and safe, along with its similar public policy of giving lip service to patriotism.

After all, who could find fault with being in support of children and their chance to be educated, to have doors of opportunity opened for them? As a result of Masonry's consistent, ongoing public relations efforts in this regard, the public, when thinking of what Masonry stands for, thinks of that dedicated teacher with an apple on her desk, Old Glory hanging on the wall, "God Bless America" painted over the door, and a room full of happy, growing children feasting on knowledge.

Good public relations, I thought, and left it at that. Later on in my studies of Freemasonry, I learned that support of public schools is also a matter of emphasis in the Order of DeMolay. In this prep school for the lodge, the Masonic Order for boys not yet twenty-one (the minimum age for joining the lodge itself), the DeMolay boys in their black, hooded, Dracula-style robes declare in the opening ceremony of their lodge their support of the public schools exclusively.[2]

Interesting, I thought, there is that public school angle again. And, they must say "exclusively." This made me think that there must be more to Freemasonry's support of public schools than merely a matter of shallow public image building, but I still had no idea of the motive or the depth of their commitment.

Freemasonry and the New Age

Still later in my Masonic studies, a friend called my attention to the fact that the late Alice Bailey, most revered of New Age writers, had made an interesting statement in her book *Externalisation of the Hierarchy*.[3] She wrote that there were three main channels by means of which the American people will be prepared to receive and accept the New Age messiah, Lord Maitraya.

These three channels would be the traditional religious system (which translates to the dead church system), Freemasonry, and the public schools. My mind seized upon the Freemasonry part because it was such an important bit of evidence tying Masonry to the New Age and its neo-pagan revival.

The dead church angle made sense immediately. It is common knowledge that more and more traditional churches and their educational institutions, having long since abandoned the experiential reality of the Christian faith and belief in the Bible, are dabbling in the New Age (or converting outright). For example, not long ago there was a ripple in the news about a witchcraft seminar conducted by the theological seminary of Southern Methodist University in which a neo-pagan instructor built an altar to the goddess Diana and had the students offer sacrifices to her.

Such dabbling of the dead church system in the New Age was not news to me: once the unchanging standard of Holy Scripture is first doubted and then abandoned, such occult drifting is entirely predictable. But, here again was the public schools thing.

Interesting, I again thought. But, I just assumed that she meant something subtle like slipping a little occult poison into otherwise wholesome textbooks and materials. My attention was focused on the Freemasonry aspect of her statement, for that was what was on my mind. I had still not realized the fundamental importance to these groups of keeping children in the public schools and the consequent threat to them represented by Christian schools, private academies, and home schooling.

Alice Bailey had much, much more in mind than just mixing a little of the occult in with essentially traditional books and materials, but I failed even to suspect it. I had not yet seen the public school connection.

Mormonism Too

Then, recently, a copy of a secret Mormon document, a handout at a leadership conference in Utah, shed more light on the subject.[4] The subject of the conference was troublemakers within Mormonism, those who might cause problems by thinking independently rather than blindly following the ever-changing and many contradictory pronouncements and positions of the Mormon hierarchy, the leadership elite.

There were twenty warning signs the leaders were told to watch for. Number one on the list was "They follow the practice of home schooling." Since, for Mormons, Christian schools are not an option, this translates in most cases to "They will not keep their children in public schools." Since Mormonism cannot be truly separated from Freemasonry and since neither can be separated from the New Age, this rang a very loud bell! Mormonism is also committed to public schools! But, why? I had still not seen the public school connection.

The Public Education Reform Movement

Three years ago, public school reform hit Kentucky like a great tidal wave. Before the citizens of the commonwealth had any idea of what was happening, let alone what it meant, they were overwhelmed. Their historic public school system, with its local control in the form of elected members of the local school board, was gone. The public school program, its goals and methods, had been radicalized, and control belonged to the state.

My wife, suspicious from the start of the promotional materials produced by the state, began to ask questions; the answers were disturbing. Similarly, my very first exposure to the state's program set off alarms in me. With no knowledge of all this, and with absolutely no preconceived ideas, I didn't like the sound of a state-sponsored radio promotional spot about the new program. It quoted an old African proverb to the effect that "It takes a whole village to raise a child." I thought, "This sounds anti-family and unscriptural to me. It is saying that the parents, the family alone, can't be trusted with the rearing of the child and that we need the state's help." I thought, "Since when do we need to regulate American social and educational institutions on the basis of African proverbs?"

With every question, every discovery, the reform program was revealed as un-American, unscriptural, and anti-traditional in its goals and practices. There was a great deal more there than the public had been told, and it all looked bad. Once again, the education bureaucrats were reinventing the wheel, and, as usual, it wasn't round. But, this was much worse; this time they were after total revision of our values, our social and political system; they were after the surrender of our personal freedom and privacy in the guise of concern for child welfare. George Orwell's "Big Brother" had arrived, and most of us didn't even know he was coming!

Kentucky Has Become the Showpiece

For the radical social manipulators, Kentucky had become the focus, the chosen battleground for their breakthrough, and they had concentrated all the weapons they had in the assault. There had been several years of low-profile planning sessions and an advertising campaign that presented right-sounding goals.

The total effect of the promotion was deceptive and dishonest, and most citizens were completely unaware of the impending changes. Those who were at all aware of it generally believed that it was merely a program to improve academics, to raise standards of student performance, to improve literacy, and get back to basics. Nothing could have been further from the truth! In fact, its true purposes were exactly the opposite. When "D Day" came, the members of the legislature were presented with a nine-hundred page bill, the Kentucky Education Reform Act (KERA), nine days before the vote.

As a result of intense lobbying, even more intense political arm twisting, and record-breaking sums of money from the pork barrel, most of them voted for the bill without even reading it. KERA became the law in Kentucky; the traditional education system was history; local control was gone; Big Brother had arrived; and most Kentuckians, including the legislators, didn't even know it.

The New World Order Agenda

The minds, money, and political power behind the movement to overhaul Kentucky's (and all other states') public schools are the same ones behind the overall push toward the New World Order, with its one-world, Socialist government and its one-world, New Age religion.

As a result of secret planning and collusion by governors of key states, principally Bill Clinton [then] of Arkansas, Wallace Wilkinson of Kentucky, Lamar Alexander of Tennessee, Jim Hunt of North Carolina, and Thomas Kean of New Jersey, the push is now on to get all state legislatures to enact the program.

The real power behind the movement is, and has been for a century, the Carnegie Foundation. Working with it are the Rockefeller Foundation, the Ford Foundation, and the teachers' unions (the NEA [National Educa-

tion Association] and the AFT [American Federation of
Teachers]). The primary training grounds for education
activists have been colleges of education in left-leaning
universities, particularly Teacher's College of Columbia
University.

Key leaders and doctrinal idols have included such as
John Dewey, father of modern education and co-author
of *The Humanist Manifesto*; George Counts, associate of
John Dewey at Columbia and author of *Dare the Schools
Create a New Social Order?*; New Age prophetess Alice
Bailey; Marilyn Ferguson, author of *The Aquarian Con-
spiracy*; and globalist educators Robert Muller and Dor-
othy J. Maver.

Behind it all, thinly concealed, can be found the leaders of the Council on Foreign Relations with its international bankers and global manipulators, the very same
people who control the key tax-exempt foundations. Many
of these men are Freemasons; many are humanists. Not
one is known to be an evangelical Christian.

These immensely powerful men (and women) really
do believe that they alone know what is best for the world
and that it is only right that they and their friends, the
cultural elite, should rule the world. And, they intend to
rule the world using the machinery of the United Nations.

Cooperating happily are the major news media, controlled by the same people, progressively molding public
perceptions. The only real obstacle to their plan is that
most Americans don't want to give up American independence, cancel the Constitution, abolish the Bible, and
accept rule by a God-rejecting, one-world, socialist dictatorship which will tell them what to do and what to think,
monitoring and recording everything they say and do.
The American people aren't fools.

In order for these Socialist manipulators to have any
hope of success in bringing to pass their goals of global
control, they must somehow eliminate traditional values
and independent thinking in the general population and
replace them with the ideals of global socialistic dictatorship. God, family, and country must somehow be replaced

by New Age paganism, state control of children, and the global community.

These dreamers and schemers have known from the beginning that their goals could not be reached quickly, that it would take several generations to gradually weaken traditional values and then replace them. They have been patient, taking pleasure in their gradual progress; however, it appears that they are now mobilizing for the final assault, and they smell victory.

These education reform programs have been introduced in bits and pieces for over a century, creating and promoting educational fads, rewriting history, discrediting the wisdom of the Founding Fathers, and picking away at our foundational beliefs and national sovereignty. But, now they intend to bring it all together by the year 2000. All the big guns have been rolled out, all their resources are being mobilized, and the final push is on— nationwide. Their program is law, or is becoming law, in several states.

Quietly, powerfully, and contrary to the Constitution, it is also moving through the U.S. Congress as proposed legislation for the entire nation in both the House and Senate. On the day of this writing, in late 1993, in the House of Representatives, it is called "Parents as Teachers"; in the Senate, the Bush Administration's "America 2,000" program is now called "Goals 2,000."

The School Reform Program in Summary

Under the reform program, the public schools would teach globalism, denounce national sovereignty, reject absolute standards of right and wrong, de-emphasize scholastic achievement, and emphasize right attitudes (e.g., accepting all lifestyles and occult, New Age religions as normal and good). Individual thinking and achievement will be out; group thinking and cooperative living will be in.

The teacher will no longer teach, becoming merely a facilitator, allowing the children to decide what they will do and how they will do it. Traditional classrooms and grade levels will be abolished from preschool through high school. All children will be considered mentally ill at the outset, and all will undergo psychotherapy; there will be a mental health clinic in each school. Traditional achievement tests, to measure academic knowledge, will be replaced by assessment tests which will evaluate attitudes and beliefs.

Extensive computerized records (portfolios) will be kept on each child's attitudes and beliefs, along with snooping files on the beliefs and attitudes of their parents and teachers. A social worker will be assigned to each child at birth, will bond with him, teach the parents how to rear the child, and will closely observe the child in the home to watch for any wrong beliefs or actions by parents. Disciplining of the child will not be tolerated. Parents with old-fashioned ideas of right and wrong, Bible beliefs, etc., can have their children taken away by the state on the basis of emotional child abuse (spanking) in the home.

In the name of freeing the children to think for themselves, they will instead be indoctrinated with darkness and confusion controlled by the state. Their parents, if they attempt to train them up in the way they should go, to rear them in the nurture and admonition of the Lord, will be made criminals.

Aside from the unscriptural, un-American nature of all this, none of it has ever been tested, yet alone demonstrated to be an improvement. The enormous cost, of course, will be borne by the parents. As they have their children and their family lives taken away from them, they will at the same time have to assume the crushing tax burden necessary to pay for it all. Education bureaucrats, social workers, mental health clinics, and huge computerized record systems don't come cheap.

Finally, It All Made Sense

Once I saw that the same people behind the New World Order and its New Age occult religion are, and have been all along, behind the current movement to radicalize the public schools, it all made sense. I saw that the only hope they could ever have to cause Americans to accept their radical socialist dictatorship would be to control the education and values of at least one generation of children, having eliminated the influence of parents and their traditional values.

An entire generation, indoctrinated, watched, and controlled by them, is what they must have in order to succeed. This is why they have been infiltrating the public schools for so long, and this is why they oppose Christian schools, private academies, and home schooling. If the children aren't in the public school system, they can't be indoctrinated and controlled. It's just that simple.

The Public School Connection

This, then, is the public school connection. This is why Freemasonry, with its New Age vision for a one-world religion of neo-pagan nature worship, promotes public schools exclusively. This is what New Age prophetess Alice Bailey clearly saw. This is what Mormon leaders, with their Masonic roots and affiliation and their New Age vision for a one-world theocracy, clearly see. This, dear friend of truth, is the public school connection. I may be wrong, but, if there is a better explanation, I haven't found it.

I Couldn't Have Summarized It Better!

In the September 1950 issue of *New Age Magazine*, that most influential and prestigious of Masonic journals, all this was summarized perfectly. In his article "God's Plan in America" C. William Smith wrote the following:

> As stated before, God's Plan in America is a nonsectarian plan. Our Constitution is non-sectarian. Our great American Public Schools . . . God's chosen schools . . . are nonsectarian. The Great Spirit behind this great nation is nonsectarian. Our great American Public Schools have never taken away from any child the freedom of will, freedom of spirit or freedom of mind. That is the divine

reason that Great God our King has chosen the Great American Public Schools to pave the way for the new race, the new religion and the new civilization that is taking place in America.

Any mother, father or guardian who is responsible for the taking away of freedom of mind, freedom of will or freedom of spirit is the lowest criminal on this earth, because they take away from that child the God-given right to become a part of God's great plan in America for the dawn of the New Age of the world.

What could be more plain? What more could be said to convince you?

Endnotes

1. Henry C. Clausen, *Why Public Schools?* (Washington: Supreme Council, 33°, Southern Jurisdiction, 1979), 1-79. Clausen is a Thirty-third Degree Mason of The Supreme Council and a Thirty-third Degree Mason of the Mother Council of the World. See also *Reasons for Joining the Scottish Rite, Reunion Program, Scottish Rite Temple* (Miami: 1966).

2. Interview with Harmon R. Taylor, Past Grand Chaplain, Grand Lodge of New York, 5 June 1993, *HRT Ministries Newsletter* (Third Quarter 1990).

3. Alice A. Bailey, *The Externalisation of the Hierarchy* (New York, NY: Lucis Press, 1957) 510-512. See also letter from Tara Center, North Hollywood, California (Marilyn Wilzbach), 9 July 1987, to Kieth Harris (Omega Publishers), Marion, KY.

4. Handout: "Profile of the splinter Group Members or Others with Troublesome Ideologies, southern Utah Leadership Conference (LDS) on Dealing with Apostate and Splinter Groups."

Three

Freemasonry and the New Age World Religion

Dick Smith

Machu Picchu in the Andes

As she watched the flickering candle, she felt herself becoming one with the flame. Suddenly, across the spring in the darkened cavern, she saw David surrounded by shimmering lights. Even more amazing were the vibrating auras she saw dancing around the vegetation on the shore of the underground grotto.

All at once she felt herself leaving her body! She floated through the top of the cave and swept up through the clouds and on beyond the earth itself to the moon. Trailing behind her she saw a thin silver cord. On past the moon she went, and, on the other side, far out in the darkness of space, she saw a nebula. She wondered if her silver cord would reach that far, and, with that limiting thought, she felt herself begin traveling back down to earth and on back into her body.

As I viewed Shirley MacLaine's graphic portrayal of her first occult out-of-body experience, I was truly sickened at heart. I knew millions of others were also watching that January night back in 1987 as ABC broadcast the second of a two-part mini-series based on the famous movie star's book *Out on a Limb*.

Uncounted thousands were being suckered into the New Age by this slick recruiting effort orchestrated by the PR firm of Lucifer and associates. A few minutes earlier, they had seen her guru, David Manning, driving his truck down a dark mountain road near Machu Picchu in the Andes. As they careened down the narrow, winding road, David's eyes had been closed and his hands off the wheel! He later explained to a shaken Shirley that Mayan, his out-of-this-world girl friend—a visitor who had arrived on Flying Saucer Express from the distant star cluster of the Pleiades—had been driving the truck through remote control using the "God Energy."

Who can forget the earlier, pathetic scene which shows Shirley and David standing on the shore of the Pacific shouting at the waves, "I am God!" David finally confesses to Shirley that several months previously Mayan had commissioned him to recruit Shirley as a spokesperson for the "truths" she was learning about the New Age and the occult. As a world-famous movie star, Shirley's influence would be of immense value to the plan of the "Masters of Wisdom."

What this plan is really designed to accomplish was certainly not revealed that night. Nor was it revealed in Shirley's book. But, the demons behind it have revealed parts of their plan to others in the New Age. A plan to establish a new world government and a New Age world religion. It will be, as we'll see, the kingdom of the Anti-Christ, and Freemasonry will be at its core.

Masonry's "Royal Secret"

On page 861 of *Morals and Dogma of the Ancient and Accepted Scottish Rite of Freemasonry*, "prepared for the Supreme Council of the Thirty-third Degree, for the Southern Jurisdiction of the United States, and Published by its Authority" in 1871, Albert Pike, Masonry's most distinguished authority, concludes his lengthy and authoritative work with these words:

The Royal Secret, of which you are a Prince, if you are a true adept . . . is that which the Sohar [a book of the Kabalah] terms The Mystery of the Balance. It is the Secret of the Universal Equilibrium. . . . Such, my Brother, is the True Word of a Master Mason; such the true Royal Secret, which makes possible, and shall at length make real, the Holy Empire of true Masonic Brotherhood. (Albert Pike, *Morals and Dogma* [Richmond: L.H. Jenkins, Inc., 1924], 861)

This statement discloses the ultimate goal of Masonry: to establish what Pike calls a "Holy Empire." This "empire" is to be a one-world government; it will be "holy" because it will be ruled by the princes of the New Age world religion. This New World Order, Pike says, will be the "true Masonic Brotherhood."

The God of Philosophy

Manley P. Hall, Thirty-third Degree, was called "Masonry's Greatest Philosopher," according to his obituary carried in the Thirty-third Degree Council's publication, *The Scottish Rite Journal*, in November 1990. "Illustrious Manley Palmer Hall," as they called him, "received the Scottish Rite's highest honor, the Grand Cross, in 1985 because of his exceptional contributions to Freemasonry," they wrote.

In his book *Lectures on Ancient Philosophy*, published in 1929, Hall indicates that he, like Pike, sees the "philosophic elect" of Freemasonry as the future rulers of a new world empire. He states that Masonry has yet a "great work" to do, that of ringing in the New Age, a "more glorious day," which is at hand. He says a "new day is dawning for Freemasonry." Men are now turning away from "the insufficiency of theology and the hopelessness of materialism" and "in this new era wherein the old order is breaking down," men are finally turning to seek "the god of philosophy."

This will ring in the rule of the philosophic elect and result in the reorganization of society, undoubtedly along Masonic lines. He adds:

By thus doing his part in the reorganization of
society, the workman may earn his "wages" as all
good Masons should. A new light is breaking in
the East, a more glorious day is at hand. The rule
of the philosophic elect—the dream of the ages—
will yet be realized and is not far distant. To her
loyal sons, Freemasonry sends this clarion call:
"Arise ye, the day of labor is at hand; the Great
Work awaits completion. . . ." [They are] the Master
Craftsmen of the universe! (Manley P. Hall, *Lectures on Ancient Philosophy* [Los Angeles: The Hall
Publishing Co., 1929], 417)

The New Age-Masonic Connection

While I've never been a Mason, until 1976 I was involved in the same occult philosophy, or "Secret Doctrine," which lies at the root of both Freemasonry and the
New Age movement. I had long been aware of the occult
nature of Masonry. But, back in 1987, while doing extensive research into the works of New Agers and other
occultists for an article on the New Age movement, I was
struck by their frequent statements about Masonry.

As we look at how Freemasonry is to help restore the
occult mystery religions and initiation ceremonies of
ancient times, keep in mind that nearly all those in Masonry and the New Age movement are involved for what
they think are good motives. Unfortunately, they are being
deceived by one "who appears, as it were, as an angel of
light."

But, is there really a connection between Freemasonry and the New Age movement, as we claim? If so,
what is this connection? What are the characteristics of
the coming New Age world religion? Is Masonry really
based on occult, mystic rites of ancient, pagan mystery
religions? What role is Freemasonry to play in the unveil-
ing of the New Age world system? To answer these questions, we'll look to the authorities of both Masonry and
the New Age movement.

The New Age Queen

Alice A. Bailey is well known to anyone who has even only a slight knowledge of the New Age movement. She has been called "The New Age Queen." Indeed, she is the key figure of this century in disclosing details of the plan to institute on earth the rule of the so-called Masters of Wisdom.

Details of this plan were unveiled to Helena Petrovena Blavatsky who wrote *Isis Unveiled* and *The Secret Doctrine* in the latter part of the last century. H.P.B., as she's called for short (for obvious reasons) also founded the Theosophical Society. These books were supposedly "transmitted" to her by mental telepathy from one of the "Masters of Wisdom" of the Great White Brotherhood, Djwhal Khul, or "DK." This is the same demon—masquerading as a "Master"—who gave Alice A. Bailey her revelations in this century. (We'll learn more about H.P.B and DK shortly.)

As the recipient of DK's telepathic transmissions in the first half of this century, Alice Bailey wrote many books on a variety of occult topics relating to the unfolding of "The Plan."

A key part of this plan calls for establishing a new world religion which is to be based on the mystery religions of ancient Babylon, Egypt, Greece, Rome, and other pagan nations of the past. Alice A. Bailey explains for us their origin and significance:

> These ancient mysteries were originally given to humanity by the Hierarchy, and were—in their turn—received by the Hierarchy from the Great White Lodge on Sirius. They contain the clue to the evolutionary process, hidden in number and words. . . . They veil the secret of man's origin and destiny. (Alice A. Bailey, *The Rays and the Initiations* [New York: Lucis Publishing Co., 1955], 330. Also excerpted in a compilation of selections from her works, *Ponder on This* [New York: Lucis Publishing Co., 1980], 15)

We'll look at the New Age concepts of "the Hierarchy," and, yes, you read it right—a Masonic lodge on the star Sirius—shortly. But, first, let's get a better understanding of something that will play a major role in the coming New Age world religion—the "Mysteries," or mystery religions. Mystery religions are defined by the *New Columbia Encyclopedia* (4th ed.) as,

> in Greek and Roman religion, some important secret cults. . . . Although the mystic rites were kept secret, it was known that they required elaborate initiations, including . . . accepting occult knowledge, and acting out a sacred drama. . . . Since the mystery deities were associated primarily with fertility, many scholars believe that these cults were based on unrecorded primitive fertility rites.

Of course, Satan's true goal regarding what Bailey has hinted at as man's "destiny" is to enslave him in his one-world religion and his visible, or "externalized," kingdom on the earth, which will restore to mankind these mysteries, including their "sacred drama."

Man's Godhood

To some, talking about Satan as if he actually existed is a sign of mental retardation. But, New Agers who write about visitors from space and Masonic lodges on Sirius are not psychos, but are among the world's elite. People such as H.G. Wells, Buckminister Fuller, Norman Cousins, Dr. Carlos Romulo, Theodore M. Hesburgh, John Denver, Robert Heilbroner, Alvin Toffler, Mohandas Gandhi, U. Thant, Robert Mueller, and Shirley MacLaine are not (or were not) exactly street people. Their strange beliefs put them in agreement with hundreds of millions of others in the Eastern religions of the world.

These New Agers believe that man is about to experience a new step in evolution. As a new, "higher" life form, he will need a new religious system in which to express this next stage on his way to godhood. To accomplish this, Eastern and Western religions are converging, they believe, and a new one-world religion (a synthesis of the two systems) is just over the horizon. This new religion will be based on the mysticism of the great Eastern religions.

But, New Agers aren't the only ones promoting this concept! So are top Freemasons! Henry Clausen, former Sovereign Grand Commander of the Supreme Council, Thirty-third Degree, Mother Council of World Freemasonry, is one who also has proclaimed this idea. In *Emergence of the Mystical*, written while he was the highest Mason in the land, he talks about the coming New Age and its relationship with the mysticism of Eastern religions. He states:

> Today we are at the threshold of a new era. All signs point to this fact. . . . We look toward a transformation into a New Age using, however, the insight and wisdom of the ancient mystics. . . . This new world view is emerging because there has been a recent correlation between modern physics and the mysticism of Eastern religions. (Henry C. Clausen, *Emergence of the Mystical* [The Supreme Council 33rd Degree, Ancient and Accepted Scottish Rite of Freemasonry, Southern Jurisdiction, U.S.A., 1981], 19)

Before continuing, let's make sure we understand exactly what this term "mysticism" means. According to the *New Columbia Encyclopedia*, mysticism is "the practice of . . . magic, occultism, or the esoteric. . . . Included in the mystic tradition were the Hermetic philosophers and the Alchemists." A mystic is "one who practices mysticism, i.e., magic, occultism, witchcraft."

Now go back and reread Clausen's statement, perhaps now with a little more enlightenment. Keep these definitions in mind. You'll encounter them constantly in New Age and Masonic writings. It is not surprising to find high initiates—the princes and adepts—of Freemasonry promoting New Age ideas. Indeed, New Age authorities refer frequently to Freemasonry and its role down through the centuries in preserving the occult mystery religions of ancient days and so do the leaders of Freemasonry.

That Ol' Time Religion

The revival of this "ol' time religion" is, of course, being touted as a "religion for a New Age." But, it has an old familiar ring—or should we say "smell"—to it: the smell of sulfur!

This "new" religion is, in fact, as old as the Garden of Eden, where Satan brought about the fall of man. It flowered at Babylon, bloomed in Egypt with the sun god Osiris and the moon goddess Isis, and is alive today in the Hindu religion, other Eastern religions, and Western religions such as Unity, Christian Science, Unitarianism, New Thought, Spiritualism, and Mormonism. It also lives on in the lodges, dogma, and rites of Freemasonry.

I'm sure very few new Masons have realized that they were being initiated into an organization which—in spite of its recent public relations pronouncements to the contrary—considers itself the present day embodiment of these mystery religions. But that this is the case is attested to by numerous New Agers and Masonic scholars, including Alice A. Bailey's husband, Foster, a Thirty-third Degree Mason.

> Masonry is the descendent of, or is founded upon, a divinely imparted religion which long antedates the prime date of creation as given in our Bible. [It] is all that remains to us of the first world religion which flourished in an antiquity so old that it is impossible to affix a date. It was the first unified world religion. . . . To this, such symbols as the pyramids, both in Egypt and South America, bear witness. . . . The ancient Mysteries were temporary custodians of the ancient truth and closely allied to the Masonic work of today. . . . The relation of the Mysteries to Masonry has oft been recognized, and the golden thread of living continuity can be traced through them to modern Ma-

sonry. The Mysteries . . . are all parts of that ancient thread which has its origin in that primeval religion which terminates today in Masonry. (Foster Bailey, *The Spirit of Masonry* [Kent, England: Lucis Press Ltd, 1957], 30-2)

Masonry is regarded as the direct descendant, or as a survival of the mysteries . . . of Isis and Osiris in Egypt. . . . (Robert Freke Gould, *History of Freemasonry* [New York, 1884], 1:13)

The signs, symbols and inscriptions date from . . . the Sumerian civilizations. . . , Chaldea [Babylon], Assyria, Greece, Rome and even in Mexico and Yucatan. . . . Some rites of the Scottish Rite of Freemasonry of our Mother Jurisdiction have been in existence from time immemorial. For we teach the same grand truths, the same sublime philosophies . . . as those adepts of the ancient mysteries taught in their esoteric rites. (Henry C. Clausen, *Messages for a Mission* [The Supreme Council 33°, A & ARFM, Mother Jurisdiction of the World, 1971], 5-7)

Note that Clausen, when he was the highest Mason in the land, stated unequivocally that "we teach the same grand truths, the same sublime philosophies . . . as those adepts of the ancient mysteries taught in their esoteric rites." The New Age movement and Masonry are the major vehicles Lucifer is using to bring about his externalized kingdom on earth, which will be a revival of the mystery religions of Babylon and other ancient nations.

These occult doctrines of mystery of Babylon can be traced back to the period after the flood when Babylon's first king, Nimrod, and his queen, Semiramis, established the mystery religion that spread into Persia, Egypt, Greece, and other nations, which set up secret brotherhoods of initiated magicians and priests. They worshiped the sun and the moon as the universal principles of generation. The sun was the male, or active principle, and the moon the female, or passive principle. These were symbolized by the sexual organs of the male and female—and their sexual union. This pagan phallic worship was central to the universal religion practiced by virtually all mankind in ancient days.

As part of the initiation rites for their temple worship, all these nations celebrated a common mystery drama, perhaps with different names and stories, but with a similar plot.

Mystery Play of the Sun and the Moon

This drama told about the death of an individual (who represented the sun) at the hands of three ruffians (the three winter months); the cutting into parts of the body and the dispersion of these body parts; the search by the wife (representing the moon), who found all the parts except the phallus; her substituting a wooden phallus for the lost one; and his (the sun's) resurrection at the vernal equinox.

This story—the Isis legend—was part of the general religion practiced by mankind in ancient days: a pagan, nature religion—the worship of the sun, moon, and starry hosts. According to the highest Masonic authorities, this is the same story preserved down to this day in the symbols and rites of Freemasonry!

The plot of the Masonic version is part of the initiation ceremony for the Third, or Master Mason, Degree. It involves the supposed death of Hiram Abiff—who is said to have built Solomon's Temple—at the hands of three ruffians; a search for his body; the loss of a "secret word"; and the substitution of a new word for the "lost" one. This new word is an amalgamation of the names of three sun gods and thus relates to the active (or male) principle, i.e., the phallus. At the climax of the drama, Hiram is resurrected to new life.

The New Age movement seeks to restore to all mankind this mystery play along with the process of initiation—initiation into a New Age. A Luciferic initiation which will, they say, take place in Masonic temples as part of the New Age world religion, which will restore the ancient mysteries.

Today, according to Freemasonry's most distinguished
authorities, the occult secrets of these mystery religions
are embedded in the symbols and rites of Freemasonry.
If this is true, it follows that Freemasonry, itself, must be
a religion. If Freemasonry is a religion, what kind of
religion is it?

Masonic Authorities

Chief among Freemasonry's distinguished authorities
is Albert Pike. Before looking at what Pike said about
this, we should point out that, despite what Masonic leaders claim today—that Pike is just one of many Masonic
writers of the past and deserves no special attention—the
truth is that Pike was, and is, Scottish Rite Masonry's
highest authority. The word *authority* is based on the word
author, and Pike is the one who authored the Scottish Rite
as practiced today.

Joseph Fort Newton, one of this centuries' most noted
Masonic authorities, in his book *The Builders*, captions a
full page picture of Pike with these words:

> Sovereign Grand Commander of the Supreme
> Council, 33°, Ancient and Accepted Scottish Rite,
> Southern Jurisdiction, U.S.A. from 1859 to his
> death in 1891. He recast the old Scottish Rite ritu-
> als and brought them to their present state of
> beauty and perfection. (Joseph Fort Newton, *The
> Builders* [Richmond, VA: Macoy Publishing and Sup-
> ply Co., Inc., 1944], 16a)

Note that he states Pike brought the rituals "to their
present state of . . . perfection." In addition, Pike was an
honorary member of virtually every Grand Lodge on earth.
He is the only Masonic authority to be given the honor
of being entombed in the House of the Temple in Washington, D.C. Manly P. Hall, in his book *Lectures on Ancient
Philosophy*, quotes another high ranking Mason who eulogized Pike.

> To Pike the following remarkable tribute was paid
> by Sterling Kerr, Jr., 33°, Deputy for the Inspector-

General for the District of Columbia, upon crown-
ing with laurel the bust of Pike in the House of the
Temple: "Pike was an oracle greater than that of
Delphi. He was Truth's minister and priest. His
victories were those of peace. Long may his memory
live in the hearts of the Brethren."

Then, Hall adds some high praise of his own, stating
that Pike was single-handedly responsible for making
Freemasonry the most powerful organization in America:

Affectionately termed "Albertus Magnus" by his
admirers, Pike wrote of Hermeticsm and alchemy
and hinted at the Mysteries of the Temple. Through
his zeal and unflagging energy, American Freemasonry was raised from comparative obscurity to
become the most powerful organization in the land.
(Hall, 414)

So much for the claim that Albert Pike's works are
not really authoritative! I'll state it again: Pike is the authority on the Scottish Rite, he's the one who wrote it! He
also wrote the book containing the philosophy which
underlies the Scottish Rite, *Morals and Dogma.*

What did Albert Pike say about Masonry as a religion? This is an important question. Since we are saying
that Freemasonry is to be at the core of the New Age
world religion, it's obvious that Freemasonry, itself, must
be clearly seen to be a religion.

Masonry Is a Religion

But, the claim is being made repeatedly today by the
Thirty-third Degree Council that Freemasonry is not a
religion. But, could we expect to get the truth about these
matters from any Mason? For, every Mason has sworn
upon penalty of his own death not to reveal secrets of the
order to anyone who is "not entitled to them." To do so
would bring upon this Mason a death sentence according
to his own sworn oaths.

Indeed, most Masons will loudly deny their brotherhood is a religion. This is especially true of Masons who

profess to be Christians. To settle this question, let's look at what Masonry's highest authorities state about this issue.

In *Morals and Dogma of the Ancient and Accepted Scottish Rite of Freemasonry*, Grand Commander and Prince Adept Albert Pike clearly identifies Freemasonry as an occult religion, the universal religion of all mankind since the beginning of time. He says, "Every Masonic Lodge is a temple of religion; and its teachings are instructions in religion."[1]

Before looking at what else Pike had to say about Masonry as a religion, let's establish the authority of another of these men, Albert G. Mackey. Frequently when we quote figures such as Pike and Mackey, some Masons respond with something like, "Well, that's just their opinion. Anyway, I never heard of these guys before."

After a recent appearance on a ninety minute radio call-in show in Orlando, for example, I had about forty calls after the show, many from Masons. One of them wanted to know where I got all the information I was quoting. I told him from Albert G. Mackey and Albert Pike and asked him if he'd ever heard of them. He said he thought he'd heard of Mackey but didn't recognize Pike's name. After I mentioned that Pike had written *Morals and Dogma*, he suddenly remembered that he had the book, but "it's put away somewhere. It'd take a year to read that thing!" Another Mason called and stated, "I'm probably the only man alive who has read Pike through twice."

But, these two Masonic writers, over the past one hundred years, have been the major authorities recognized worldwide by Freemasonry. However, today many rank-and-file Masons say they've never heard of Albert Pike or Albert G. Mackey. The typical Mason, if he reads any Masonic materials at all, gets much of his information about Masonry from a section in his Masonic Bible containing questions and answers on Masonry. This typical Mason never bothers looking further into what the organization believes in the more esoteric areas.

In fact, the introduction to this section of the Masonic Bible, called "Questions and Answers, One Hundred and Sixty Questions and Answers . . . Pertaining to the Symbolism of Masonry and its Connection with the Bible," states: "The following questions and answers are intended to convey to the average Mason the information every Mason desires without taking the time to do the research."[2]

The interesting point here is that, according to the credit line, which is part of the title of this section of the Masonic Bible, the source for this information is a name most Masons claim they've never heard of. It reads: "compiled from the works of Albert G. Mackey." So, these "average" Masons who say they've never heard of Mackey, but who accept this section of the Masonic Bible as authoritative, do not realize that this authority is based primarily on the authority of Mackey!

Mackey Says Masonry a Religion But Not Christianity

Indeed, Dr. Albert G. Mackey literally "wrote the book" on Freemasonry; he is the author of the *Encyclopedia of Freemasonry* published in 1879. Mackey was Past General High Priest and Secretary General of the Supreme Council Thirty-third Degree for the Southern Jurisdiction of the U.S., which takes in thirty-five of the fifty states. He spent more than ten years writing this encyclopedia. It has been considered one of the top two authoritative works on Masonry. (The other is Albert Pike's *Morals and Dogma*.)

In this encyclopedia, Mackey clearly identifies Freemasonry as a religion, and he categorically states that it is not Christianity:

> Freemasonry is a religious institution, and hence its regulations inculcate the use of prayer as a proper tribute of gratitude to the beneficent Author of life. (Albert Mackey, *Encyclopedia of Freemasonry* Vol. 2 [Chicago, New York, London: The Masonic History Co., 1924], 594)

> The religion of Masonry is nonsectarian. It admits men of every creed within its hospitable bosom. It is not Judaism, though there is nothing to offend the Jew. It is not Christianity, but there is nothing in it repugnant to the faith of a Christian. (Mackey, 641)

> Freemasonry is not Christianity, nor a substitute for it. It does not meddle with sectarian creeds or doctrines, but teaches fundamental religious truth. (Mackey, 162)

Is Masonry a religion? Mackey says "yes." Is it Christian? Mackey says "no." Therefore, if Masonry is a religion and it is not the religion of Christianity, Masonry is not a Christian religion! Every Christian Mason who claims it is Christianity is either completely deceived or is a Christian in name only and needs to get saved.

Indeed, according to Billy Graham and two former presidents of the Southern Baptist Convention, up to 90 percent of our church members are not born again! Charles G. Finney, known as "the greatest preacher, theologian and evangelist of the nineteenth century," who was a Mason for a short time, stated:

> Surely, if a Mason really understood what Masonry is, as delineated in these books, no Christian Mason would think himself at liberty to remain another day in the fraternity. . . . It is as plain as possible that a man, knowing what it is, and embracing it in his heart, can not be a Christian man. To say he can is to belie the very nature of Christianity. (Charles G. Finney, *The Antichrist or the Masonic Society* [Ontario, Canada: Crown Publications, 1984], 60)

Two Religions

Let's pause for a moment to get a better understanding of the fact that there have been, and are, only two basic religions. These two are first, Paganism, which incorporates the mystery religions, Eastern religions, Freemasonry, the New Age movement, etc.; second, Judaism, which is the "mother" of both Christianity and Islam.

In his *Encyclopedia of Freemasonry*, Albert Mackey gives us a better understanding of this concept. He writes, under the heading "Paganism":

> a general appellation for the religious worship of the whole human race, except for that portion which has embraced Christianity, Judaism, or Mohammedanism. Its interest to the Masonic student arises from the fact that its principal development was the ancient mythology, in whose traditions are to be found many interesting analogies with the Masonic system.

The understanding that all religions other than Christianity, Judaism, and Islam have their common source in Lucifer's pagan, occult mystery religions, should help us place Freemasonry in its proper category. That category is definitely not in the Judeo-Christian camp!

These pagan religions and the New Age movement share the same Luciferic source as well as the same goal: establishment of a New Age world religion. Freemasonry, according to it's most distinguished authority, was "mother" to all these pagan religions!

> Much of the Masonic secret manifests itself . . . particularly to those who advance to the highest Degrees of the Ancient and Accepted Scottish Rite. That Rite raises a corner of the veil, even in the Degree of Apprentice; for it there declares that Masonry is a worship.

> It is the universal, eternal, immutable religion such as God planted in the heart of universal humanity. No creed has ever been long-lived that was not built on this foundation. . . . The ministers of this religion are all Masons who comprehend it and are devoted to it. (Pike, *Morals and Dogma*, 218–19)

As you read Pike's comments, keep in mind that they were prepared for the Southern Jurisdiction of the United

States and "published by its authority." In other words, this is the official doctrine of Freemasonry, not what some local lodge officials might claim or what the current Thirty-third Degree Council might try to lie about.

Masonry a Universal Religion

Both of Masonry's highest authorities during the past one hundred years clearly state that Masonry is a religion, complete with a religious creed—a "worship." But, just what kind of religion is Masonry?

Like Mackey, Pike says the religion of Masonry is not Christianity but is a universal religion which makes a Mason the "brother" of every other Mason on earth, bound together with these "brothers" from other religions under an "imperative obligation of a contract."

> Masonry propagates no creed except its own most simple and Sublime one; that universal religion, taught by Nature and by Reason. Its lodges are neither Jewish, Moslem, nor Christian temples. It reiterates the precepts and morality of all religions. (Pike, *Morals and Dogma*, 718-9)

> The Moral Code of Masonry is still more extensive than that developed by philosophy. To the requisitions of the law of Nature and the law of God, it adds the imperative obligation of a contract. Upon entering the Order, the Initiate binds to himself every other Mason in the world. Once enrolled among the children of Light, every Mason on earth becomes his brother. (Pike, 726)

Then, how can a Christian belong to such an organization? After all, God's Word clearly commands us not to be "yoked together with unbelievers." But, a Christian Mason "binds himself to every other Mason in the world. . . . Every Mason on earth becomes his brother."

As Finney said, any Christian who truly understands what Masonry really is could not stay another day in such a pagan cult! But, most Masons—perhaps 99 percent of them—have no conception of the true nature of their fraternity. They have never bothered to study the works of Masonry's highest authorities such as Albert Pike, Albert Mackey, and Manley P. Hall. These reveal that the organization is made up of an outer fraternity whose members are deliberately misled about Masonry's symbols and dogmas and by an occult inner brotherhood of adepts versed in magic, witchcraft, and the mystery religions of the ancient world.

Most Masons are not only unaware of the true nature of their fraternity, they have no idea they are being deliberately deceived by the craft. As admitted by Pike,

> The Blue Degrees are but the outer court or portico of the Temple. Part of the symbols are displayed there to the Initiate, but he is intentionally misled by false interpretations. It is not intended that he shall understand them. Their true explication is reserved for the Adepts, the Princes of Masonry. . . . It is well enough for the mass of those called Masons, to imagine that all is contained in the Blue degrees; and whoso attempts to undeceive them will labor in vain. . . . There must always be common-place interpretations for the mass of Initiates, of the symbols that are eloquent to the Adepts. (Pike, *Morals and Dogma* 818–19)

But, Pike is not the only Masonic authority to disclose this slight-of-hand. "Illustrious" Manley P. Hall, who was eulogized by the *Scottish Rite Journal* as the fraternity's greatest philosopher, stated in his book, *Lectures on Ancient Philosophy*:

> Freemasonry is a fraternity within a fraternity—an outer organization concealing an inner brotherhood of the elect. . . , two separate yet interdependent orders, the one visible and the other invisible. . . . The invisible society is a secret and most august fraternity whose members are dedicated to the service of a mysterious arcanum arcanorum. . . , that truly secret inner society which is to the body Freemasonic what the heart is to the human body. (Hall, 397)

Masonic Magic and Witchcraft

What is this "mysterious arcanum arcanorum" which "illustrious Manley Palmer Hall" has described as being the subject of the invisible societies' dedicated service? What is the true "work" of the secret, inner organization? Pike, who wrote the Scottish Rite, and "Illustrious" Manley Hall, it's "greatest Philosopher," say that Masonry's true work is magic and witchcraft! According to Pike, "The Hermetic Science . . . embodied in certain symbols of the higher Degrees of Freemasonry, may be accurately defined as the Kabalah in active realization, or the Magic of the Works."[3]

Hall, after lamenting the fact that not all Masons are happy with this occult heritage, states that he can't see how anyone after reading Pike's great work can deny that Freemasonry is "identical" to the mystery religions:

> Even the casual observer must realize that the true wealth of Freemasonry lies in its mysticism. . . . It is quite incredible, moreover, that any initiated brother, when presented with a copy of *Morals and Dogma* upon conferment of his fourteenth degree, can read that volume and yet maintain that his order is not identical to the Mystery Schools of the first ages. (Hall, 413)

As a former occultist, I recognize much of Pike's writings as coming from the same occult revelation given to Helena Petrovna Blavatsky in *Isis Unveiled* and *The Secret Doctrine*. "Illustrious" Manley P. Hall also recognizes Pike's works as being similar to those of other occultists.

> Much of the writings of Albert Pike are extracted from the books of the French magician, Eliphas Levi, one of the greatest transcendentalists of modern times. Levi was an occultist, a metaphysician, a Platonic philosopher, who by the rituals of magic invoked even the spirit of Apollonius of Tyana, and yet Pike has inserted in his *Morals and Dogma* whole pages, and even chapters, practically verbatim. (Hall, 413-14)

Let me again point out that we're talking about a work, *Morals and Dogma*, that was prepared for and published by the greatest Masonic jurisdiction in America. In addition to Pike and Hall, Alice Bailey's husband, Foster, a Thirty-third Degree Mason, also writes about the New Age-Masonic connection as it relates to magic in his book, *The Spirit of Masonry*:

> It is the creative nature of the Masonic work . . . to work, say and think the same thing simultaneously. . . . The concentrated attention and thought power of the assembled Masons . . . is in reality a group meditation, leading to group work. . . . Masonry in its true and highest sense is magical work. . . . The effectiveness of this possible work will be paralleled by the increasing sensitivity of the race to telepathic impression. (F. Bailey, 96–98)

> Behind the magical work of the rituals must be the influence of the established rhythm. . . . The materializing upon earth of the mystical vision . . . must be brought about by the wise working of this law of rhythm and of ritual. (F. Bailey, 99)

But, wait; it gets even worse.

Pike Says Christianity Should Not Have Hated Magic

Pike has said Masonry at its core is based on the magic of the Kabalah. But, Pike says that it was necessary for this knowledge to be concealed from "the profane." He states that this "occult philosophy seems to have been the nurse or godmother of all religions, the secret lever of all the intellectual forces."

> This is what magic had been, from Zoroaster to Manes, from Orpheus to Apollonius Thayaneus; when positive Christianity, triumphing over the splendid dreams and gigantic aspirations of the school of Alexandria, publicly crushed this philosophy with its anathemas, and compelled it to

become more occult and more mysterious than ever. At the bottom of magic, nevertheless, was science. Christianity should not have hated magic, but human ignorance always fears the unknown . . .

But, since Christianity did abhor magic, the magicians resorted to inventing Masonic degrees to hide the secrets of their witchcraft:

Resorting to Masonry, the alchemists there invented Degrees, and partly unveiled their doctrine to the Initiates ... . by oral instruction afterward; for their rituals, to one who has not the key, are but incomprehensible and absurd jargon. (Pike, 730–731)[4]

Next, Pike lets the magic-hating Christians have it broadside, calling them "dunces" who sought to exterminate magic:

The dunces who led primitive Christianity astray . . . who for so many ages waged war against Magism, a war of extermination, have succeeded in shrouding in darkness the ancient discoveries of the human mind; so that we now grope in the dark to find again the key of the phenomena of nature. (Pike, 732)[5]

This is so blatant a description of Lucifer's battle with God, who declared "suffer not a witch to live," that it clearly draws the dividing line for us. On one side we have the Satanic mystery religions embedded now in the highest rites and symbols of Masonry and, on the other side, "the dunces" of Christianity.

Can any Christian member of the Masonic Order maintain that this is a Christian organization after reading this blasphemy of God?

The Great Work: Witchcraft and Magic

Among other things, Pike has just described Masonry as searching for "the key of the phenomena of nature." This is a classic definition of witchcraft. But, you need not take my word for it because Pike continues on the following pages to clearly say so.

There is in nature one most potent force, by means whereof a single man, who could possess himself of it, and should know how to direct it, could revolutionize and change the face of the world. This force was known to the ancients. It is a universal agent. . . . If science can but learn to control it, it will be possible to change the order of the seasons, to produce in night the phenomena of day, to send a thought in an instant around the world, to heal or slay at a distance, to give our words universal success, and make them reverberate everywhere.

This agent, partially revealed by the blind guesses of the disciple of Mesmer, is precisely what the Adepts of the middle ages called the elementary matter of the great work. . . . It was adored in the secret rites of the Sabbat or the Temple, under the hieroglyphic figure of Baphomet or the hermaphroditic goat of Mendes. (Pike, 734)

If you still have doubts, look up the meaning and origin of Baphomet and the goat of Mendes. They are forms of Satan, himself, and a Sabbat is "an assembly or celebration of witches or other occultists, usually held on astrologically significant days and hours."[6]

You also need to understand that the terms *witch*, *magician*, *sorcerer*, and *wizard* all mean the same thing. "A magician engages in magic, or witchcraft; the terms are synonymous."[7]

Still not convinced? Read some more of what Pike has to say about "the great work," the universal term for witchcraft.

Whoever shall learn to comprehend and execute this great work, will know great things, say the sages of the work; but whenever you depart from the centre of the Square and the Compass you will no longer be able to work with success.

Another Jewel is necessary for you, and in certain undertakings cannot be dispensed with. It is what is termed the Kabalistic pantacle. . . . This carries with it the power of commanding the spirits of the elements. (Pike, 786–7)

But, many Masons will tell you that all this talk about commanding spirits and the like is just symbolic. However, Pike cautions against reading Masonic works too quickly or believing what you may have been told that what you read is only symbolic, for, he says, that's when you are most deceived.

If you would understand the true secrets of Alchemy, you must study the works of the Masters with patience and assiduity. Every word is often an enigma; and to him who reads in haste, the whole may seem absurd. Even when they seem to teach that the great work is purification of the soul, and so to deal only with morals, they most conceal their meaning and deceive all but the initiates. (Pike, 792)

Masons also contend that Masonry is just an organization which "makes good men better," that it's all aimed at symbolically building a temple for the inward dwelling of God. But, if this is your belief, read again the previous statement by Pike and discern, finally, that you are a victim of deliberate deceit. Today, the Thirty-third Degree Council has even denied that Masonry is related in any way with the occult mysteries. Such a denial is preposterous on its face!

Freemasonry and the Mysteries

Here's how Pike characterized Masonry's occult heritage on page 639 of *Morals and Dogma of the Ancient and Accepted Scottish Rite of Freemasonry*: "The Occult Science of the Ancient Magi was concealed under the shadows of the Ancient Mysteries . . . and it is found enveloped in the enigmas that seem impenetrable, in the Rites of the Highest Masonry."

If the "Occult Science of the Ancient Magi[cians]" was incorporated into the "Ancient Mysteries," and, if this "Occult Science" is now "found enveloped in . . . the Rites of the Highest Masonry," then this statement by the author of the current version of those rites should be adequate to document the claim that Masonry is the repository of the occult heritage of the mysteries that are to be reinstated for the New Age world religion. This New Age world religion, we are told, is to be inaugurated by the return to earth of "the Christ."

Return of "The Christ"

Benjamin Creme is a major New Age leader, the "John the Baptist" for the New Age Christ, the Lord Maitraya, who Creme says is already in the world simply waiting for the right time to manifest his presence.

In *The Reappearance of the Christ and the Masters of Wisdom*, Creme reveals that Masonry will play an important part in the return of "the Christ" (whom Christians would call the anti-Christ), especially in the initiation ritual for the New Age religion. He states: "Through the Masonic tradition and certain esoteric groups, will come the process of initiation. In this coming age millions of people will take the first and second initiation through these transformed and purified institutions."[8]

Also, in a section of his book containing transcripts of his many lectures—including question and answer sessions—after speaking about the coming reformation of the churches and Buddhism, he is asked if he believes this reformation "will affect the various secret organizations, like the Masons, the Rosicrucians, and so on?" He answers, "Very much so. . . . The coming religion, in fact this coming age, will be dominated by . . . Magic, or Ritual, or Organization. . . . Aquarius has been called 'the implementing force of synthesis or universality,' and will bring about synthesis, universality, in the world. . . ."[9]

Note the theme of conjunction, that is, "synthesis or universality." You'll recall that Pike has said this is Masonry's "Royal Secret." You'll encounter this concept of "mixture" repeatedly in the writings of New Age and Masonic authorities.

Creme next tells us how the newly synthesized religions will be manifested.

> The new religions will manifest, for instance,
> through organizations like Freemasonry. In Free-
> masonry is embedded the core of the secret heart
> of the occult mysteries—wrapped up in number,
> metaphor and symbol. When these are
> purified. . . , these will be seen to be a true occult
> heritage. Through the Orders of Masonry, the
> Initiatory Path will be trodden and Initiation will
> be taken. (Creme, 87)

So, not only will the mystery religion be restored, but
so will the process of Initiation; and, Creme says, reiter-
ating the theme of our earlier authorities, this new religion will be universal—a conjunction of the East and West:

> A new world religion will be inaugurated which will
> be a fusion and synthesis of the approach of the East
> and the approach of the West. The Christ will bring
> together . . . Christianity and Buddhism . . . in a new
> scientific religion based on the Mysteries; on Initia-
> tion; on Invocation. . . . The very heart and core of
> the new world religion will be the esoteric process of
> Initiation. . . . Gradually, Christianity and Buddhism
> and other religions will wither away . . . as the new
> religion gains its adherents and exponents, and is
> gradually built by humanity. (Creme, 88-9)

So pervasive is the application of the universal principle of dialectics (conjunction, balance, opposites) that
Creme even says the "other religions will wither away"—
just as in Marxist theory, the state is supposed to "wither
away" and be replaced by true "Communism."

New Age Luciferic Initiation

Another of the New Age movement's major figures,
David Spangler, in *Reflections of the Christ*, reveals the true
identity of this "Christ," or Lord Maitreya. He says, "Christ
is the same force as Lucifer. . . . Lucifer works within each
of us to bring us to wholeness as we move into the New
Age."[10] Then, he tells us what kind of initiation will be
administered through the orders of Masonry: "The light
that reveals to us the path to Christ comes from

Lucifer. . . . The great initiator . . . Lucifer comes to give us the final Luciferic initiation . . . that many people in the days ahead will be facing, for it is an invitation into the New Age."[11]

So, according to top New Age leaders, the new universal religion will manifest through organizations like Masonry, and initiation into the New Age will take place in Masonic temples.

Blavatsky's Secret Doctrine and the New World Religion

But, other New Age authorities have also stated that Masonry is a universal religion and is a repository of the occult secret doctrine of the mysteries. In fact, one of the world's most occult books is loaded with references to Masonry.

Helena Petrovna Blavatsky, in her introduction to volume one of *The Secret Doctrine*, summarizes for us the nature of the secret doctrine and reveals its tie-in with Masonry.

> The Secret Doctrine was the universally diffused religion of the ancient and prehistoric world. Proofs of its diffusion. . . , together with the teaching of all its great adepts, exist to this day in the secret crypts of libraries belonging to the Occult Fraternity.
>
> There are several documents in the St. Petersburg Imperial Libraries to show that, even so late as during the days when Freemasonry, and Secret Societies of Mystics flourished unimpeded in Russia more than one Russian Mystic traveled to Tibet via the Ural mountains in search of knowledge and initiation. . . . Let anyone look over the Annals and History of Freemasonry in the archives of the Russian metropolis, and he will assure himself of the fact stated. (Helena P. Blavatsky, *The Secret Doctrine* [London: Theosophical University Press, 1888], xxxiv–vi)

We could spend much time exploring H.P.B.'s anti-Christian dogma that makes Jehovah the villain (Christians are the "Black Lodge") and Lucifer the hero (the "White Lodge"). But, we get the same doctrine in Pike's work!

Masonry's God Not Jehovah

In his discussion of the Royal Arch Degree in *Morals and Dogma*, for example, Pike reveals the true nature of Masonry's god—and, it's not Jehovah. Please, read the following slowly and carefully.

> We know that for many centuries, the Hebrews have been forbidden to pronounce the Sacred Name. . . . In India it was forbidden to pronounce the word *Aum* or *Om*, the Sacred Name of the One Deity, manifested as Brahma, Vishnu, and Seeva. . . . It was, therefore, possible for that of the name of the Deity to have been forgotten or lost. It is certain that its true pronunciation is not that represented by the word *Jehovah*; and therefore that it is not the true name of Deity, nor the Ineffable Word. (Pike, 204–5)

Pike further says that the communication of the "true nature of God" in the ancient mysteries is what we now call Masonry.

> Among all the ancient nations there was one faith and one idea of Deity for the enlightened, intelligent, and educated, and another for the common people. To this rule the Hebrews were no exception. Yehovah, to the mass of the people, was like the gods of the nations around them. . . . The Deity of the early Hebrews talked to Adam and Eve in the garden. . . . He wrestled with Jacob; he showed Moses his person, though not his face. . . . He commanded the performance of the most shocking and hideous acts of cruelty and barbarity. He hardened the heart of Pharaoh. . . . Such were the popular notions of the Deity; and

either the priests had none better, or took little
trouble to correct these notions; or the popular
intellect was not enlarged enough to enable them
to entertain any higher conceptions of the Almighty.

But such were not the ideas of the intellectual and
enlightened few among the Hebrews. It is certain
that they possessed a knowledge of the true nature
and attributes of God, as the same class of men
did among the other nations—Zoroaster, Menu,
Confucius, Socrates, and Plato. But their doctrines
on this subject were esoteric; they did not commu-
nicate them to the people at large, but only to a
favored few; and as they were communicated in
Egypt and India, in Persia and Phoenicia, in Greece
and Samonthrace, in the greater mysteries, to the
Initiates.

The communication of this knowledge and other
secrets, some of which are perhaps lost, constituted, under other names, what we now call Masonry. (Pike, 206–7)

Do we need any clearer statement than this of the
true nature of Masonry as a universal religion whose god
is not the God of the Christian and of its own character-
ization of itself as communicating the "true" attributes
and name of God, which, it emphasizes, is not Jehovah?
The god of Masonry, according to its greatest authority,
is not Jehovah! In fact, Pike states rather clearly who the
"Initiates" consider their god to be.

The Devil is the personification of Atheism or Idolatry. For the Initiates, this is not a Person, but a
Force, created for good, but which may serve for
evil. It is the instrument of Liberty or Free Will.
They represent this Force, which presides over the
physical generation, under the mythologic and
horned form of the God Pan; thence came the he-
goat of the Sabbat, brother of that Ancient Serpent, and the Light-bearer. (Pike, 102)

The same basic statement is found in Blavatsky's *Secret Doctrine*, where she ascribes the statement to Eliphas Levi, a major occultist and magician whose works, according to Manley P. Hall, Pike copied copiously.

> The Kabalists say that the true name of Satan is that of Jehovah placed upside down, for Satan is not a black god but the negation of the white deity. . . . "For the Initiates," says Eliphas Levi, "the Devil is not a person but a creative Force, for Good as for Evil." They (the Initiates) represented this Force, which presides at physical generation, under the mysterious form of God Pan—or Nature: whence the horns and hoofs of that mythical and symbolic figure, as the Christian "goat" of the Witches Sabbath. (H.P.B., 510)

The horned God Pan, or the Goat of Mendes, the he-goat of the "Witches Sabbath"—all names for the same Satanic entity—is represented in the Pentagram, the five-pointed star of witchcraft. This star is used upside down with the point at the bottom for the goat's face and beard and the two points at the top for the horns. The Pentagram is the insignia not only for witches and Satanists worldwide but also for Masons and their sister organization, Eastern Star! This goat is also called Baphomet and is the god of the twelfth century Knights Templar, ancestors of the present Masonic organization.

Clearly, the true god of the religion of the Masonic Order is not Jehovah, but Lucifer. Masonry is one of the major vehicles through which he is manifesting his ages-old attempt to take the place of God in the Universe. In fact, according to Alice A. Bailey, Lucifer actually officiated at the founding of Freemasonry! In *Initiation, Human and Solar*, Bailey writes:

> All physical plane organization—governmental, religious, or cultural—is the working out of the inner forces and causes, and, before they appear in physical manifestation, a focalization . . . of these influences and energies takes place on etheric

[spirit] levels. The organization of the Freemasons
is a case in point. . . . The Lord of the World was
the officiating agent, as is ever the case in the
founding of great and important movements. (Alice
A. Bailey, *Initiation, Human and Solar* [New York:
Lucis Publishing Co., 1970], 131-2)

Again, let us ask: how is it possible for rank-and-file
Masons—many who are professed Christians—to take part
in such a Luciferic religion? How could Christian pastors
belong to such an organization?

As Pike and Hall have admitted, Masonry is in reality
two organizations: an outer fraternity of dupes deliberately misled about Masonry's symbols and dogmas and an
occult inner brotherhood of adepts versed in magic, witchcraft and the mystery religions of the ancient world—
religions whose central tenets are being revived as the
religion of the New Age.

This is the abominable universal world religious system that the Lord Jesus Christ is returning to earth to
destroy! (See Revelation, especially chapters 17-19.)

Ancient Initiations

What did it mean to belong to these mystery religions
of ancient pagan nations that Clausen, Pike, Hall, Mackey,
and numerous other Masonic authorities say are the pre-
cursors for modern day Masonry? Let's see if we can get
a feel for what went on in those pagan initiation rites.
Please, change gears for a moment, and let your imagina-
tion run free; imagine the following scene, circa 1350
B.C.:

> *Flickering light glances off the cavernous walls and
> vaulted ceiling of the immense cave. Erie–and yet some-
> how sensuous–the torch light casts a mesmerizing spell
> on those assembled for the initiation. Their attention is
> riveted on the candidate standing on the lip of a chasm
> spanned by a swinging rope bridge. But, he stands sev-
> eral yards from the bridge, not at its entrance.*
>
> *His face is in shadow, but the rigid posture of his body
> portrays his intense concentration. His chest heaves as*

> *he breathes in and out rhythmically. Suddenly he straight-*
> *ens, and with fists clenched, raises his arms across his*
> *chest. Taking one final deep breath, he steps off the edge*
> *into the darkness. Those assembled are silent, watching*
> *intently as the candidate levitates across the chasm and*
> *steps off on the other side.*

Perhaps you may think this is more of an exercise in science fiction rather than a glimpse of what it meant to be an initiate of the mystery religions of ancient days. But, listen to "illustrious" Manley P. Hall as he describes for us the neophyte of these ages. He says that the initiate of the ancient mysteries was a man of great learning and character for whom initiation into the mysteries meant great physical trials and required great feats of occult capabilities:

> Not one Freemason out of a thousand could have survived the initiations of the pagan rites, for the tests were given in those strenuous days when men were men and death the reward for failure. The neophyte of the Druid Mysteries was set adrift in a small boat to battle with the stormy sea, and unless his knowledge of natural law enabled him to quell the storm as did Jesus upon the Sea of Galilee, he returned no more. In the Egyptian rites of Serapis, it was required of the neophyte that he cross an unbridged chasm in the temple floor. In other words, if unable by magic to sustain himself in the air without visible support, he fell headlong into a volcanic crevice, there to die of heat and suffocation. In one part of the Mithraic rites, the candidate seeking admission to the inner sanctuary was required to pass through a closed door by dematerialization. . . . (Hall, 414-5)

Hall then quotes Pike from the "Legenda for the Twenty-Eighth Degree" as stating that "the science of the Hierophants of the mysteries produced effects that to the Initiated seemed Mysterious and supernatural." (Hall, 415.)

I suppose we could all agree with Pike that levitating

across chasms, quelling storms, and passing through walls could qualify as "Mysterious and supernatural." "One Freemason out of a thousand" is probably close to the percentage of those in today's fraternity who are initiates of the secret Inner Brotherhood, who really understand the true meaning and purpose of Masonry and who practice such magic and witchcraft.

As we've seen, such magic and witchcraft have their origin in the pagan, occult mysteries of ancient days. We've also briefly touched on the belief of New Agers that all of this was given to us by the "Masters of Wisdom," or the "Hierarchy." Let's get a better understanding of this so-called Hierarchy and its role in bringing about the New Age world religion.

The Hierarchy

According to the New Age belief system, the Masters of Wisdom have ruled the affairs of the earth for millennia. They are referred to as "The Hierarchy," which is composed of advanced beings, some of whom live in an etheric (or spiritual) city over the Gobi desert called Shambala. The Hierarchy contains a range of beings all the way up to the "Lord of the World," himself.

Of course, what is being described is what the Bible clearly speaks of as the spiritual forces we are battling in the heavenly sphere, the principalities and powers of Satan's kingdom: "For your conflict is not only with flesh and blood, but also with the angels, and with powers, with the rulers of this world of darkness, and with the evil spirits under the heavens" (Eph. 6:12).

Our Lord Jesus Christ calls Satan the "Prince of the Power of the Air," and "the god of this world." In 1 John 5:19, we read that "the whole world around us is under the power of the evil one" (The Amplified Bible). In her book, *Initiation, Human and Solar*, Alice Bailey says basically the same thing.

> This Hierarchy of Brothers of Light still exists, and the work goes steadily on. They are all in physical existence, either in dense physical bodies,

such as many of the Masters employ, or in etheric
bodies, such as the more exalted helpers and the
Lord of the World occupy. . . . They exist upon
this planet with us, controlling its destinies, guid-
ing its affairs, and leading all its evolutions on to
an ultimate perfection. (A. Bailey, *Initiation*, 32)

The apostle Paul also pointed out that there are unseen spiritual beings organized in a hierarchy: "And
through him were created all things that are in heaven
and on earth, visible and invisible; whether imperial
thrones or lordships or angelic orders or dominions. . ."
(Col. 1:16). And, in 2 Corinthians 12:7, he refers to a
Satanic angel whose assignment was to attack him repeatedly (whose attacks are summarized in the previous chapter): "There was delivered to me a thorn in my flesh, the
angel of Satan, to buffet me. . . ."

So, we see that the Bible clearly states there are unseen spiritual beings in the heavenly realm, and they are
organized in a hierarchy. Alice Bailey also tells us something about the headquarters for the "Lord of the World"
in Shambala, big city in the sky.

The central home of this Hierarchy is at Shambala,
a centre in the Gobi desert, called in the ancient
books the "White Island." It exists in etheric matter. . . . Several of the Masters in physical bodies
dwell in the Himalayan mountains . . . but the
greater number are scattered all over the world,
dwelling in different places in the various nations,
unrecognized and unknown, yet forming each in
His own place a focal point for the energy of the
Lord of the World. (A. Bailey, *Initiation*, 33)

New Agers also believe that other planets are inhab-
ited and that the star Sirius is home to the Great White
Lodge from which all in this sector of the universe is
controlled. We saw earlier that, according to Bailey, this
was the source for the mysteries. These mysteries, Bailey
says, provide the secret powers for the magic and witchcraft practiced by the Hierarchy.

The Mysteries are, in reality, the true source of
revelation. . . . They concern those capacities which
enable the Members of the Hierarchy to work consciously with the energies of the planet and of the
solar system, and to control forces within the
planet. . . . The Mysteries, when restored, will make
real . . . the nature of religion, the purpose of
science, and the goal of education. These are not
what you think today. (Alice A. Bailey, *Discipleship
in the New Age* [New York, 1975], 2:15-6)

Bailey says these mysteries contain more than just
what is found in Masonry, and they will be restored more
fully when the Hierarchy (that is, the kingdom of the anti-
Christ) comes to earth visibly.

The Mysteries will be restored in other ways also,
for they contain much besides that which the
Masonic rites can reveal, or that religious rituals
and ceremonies can disclose . . . and only when
the Hierarchy is present visibly on earth, and the
Mysteries of which the Masters are the custodians
are given openly to man, will the true secret and
nature of electrical phenomena be revealed. (Ibid.)

Further, says Bailey, the churches and Masonry have
failed to do a good job in preparing the way for the
restoration of the mysteries. She writes, "The ground is
being prepared at this time for this great restoration. The
churches and Masonry are today before the judgment
seat of humanity's critical mind [because] both of them
failed in their divinely assigned tasks."[12]

So, we see that the mysteries will be restored through
the agency of liberal churches, such as Unity, Christian
Science, Mind Science, Mormonism, and others, as well
as through Masonry.

Foster Bailey Unveils the Spirit of Masonry

We've already quoted from a remarkable book, *The
Spirit of Masonry*, written by the husband of Alice A. Bailey,
Foster Bailey. In this book, we read of the true spiritual
heritage of which Masonry is the custodian. The typical

Mason reading this book—indeed, virtually anyone, Mason or not—would pass quickly over passages of great interest to one familiar with occult works such as *The Secret Doctrine* or Alice Bailey's many books, especially *Initiation, Human and Solar.*

It is of great significance that, in his introduction to part one, on page nine, Foster Bailey states: "The words used in the text of this book are the words of another." In my opinion, this is a direct reference to this book's origin from the same source as most of his wife Alice's books—as well as those of Helena Petrovena Blavatsky—that source being the Tibetan, Djwhal Khul, one of the Masters of Wisdom, who authored all these works through telepathic transmission. In other words, their source is, in reality, a demonic spirit who is a talented actor.

The interesting thing we find from reading Foster's book, which was written by a Mason for other Masons, is that the somewhat veiled references he makes to various aspects of Masonry are clearly stated, or "unveiled," in the books of his wife, Alice and those of H.P. Blavatsky. By comparing the contents of Foster's book with these others, we can clearly see the key role that Masonry has played in Satan's kingdom—in all areas of the universe.

For example, on page sixteen, in discussing the Third Degree, when he refers to the journey of the Master Mason ending in resurrection from the grave where "he enters into that great Fellowship of Master Masons who are but the expression upon earth of the divine fellowship existing in the Lodge of the Most High," we need look no further than Foster's wife, Alice, for the true explanation.

In her book, *Initiation, Human and Solar,* Alice tells us about that Lodge of the Most High—and she's not speaking of Heaven! She's speaking of the Masonic lodge on Sirius. Her comments give us a glimpse of another aspect of the close relationship between the New Age movement and Freemasonry.

> One great fact to be borne in mind is, that the initiations of the planet or of the solar system are

but preparatory initiations of admission into the greater lodge on Sirius. We have the symbolism held for us fairly well in Masonry, and in combining the Masonic method with what we are told of the steps on the Path of Holiness we get an approximate picture. [After the first four solar initiations, we get to the fifth initiation, which is] the first cosmic initiation. The fifth initiation corresponds to the first cosmic initiation, that of "entered apprentice" in Masonry; and makes a Master an "entered apprentice" of the Lodge on Sirius. The sixth initiation is analogous to the second degree in Masonry, whilst the seventh initiation makes the Adept a Master Mason of the Brotherhood on Sirius. (A. Bailey, *Initiation*, 17–8)

So, we see that Masonry is more than worldwide. When they say it's a universal religion, that's just what they mean! We see clearly that Masonry's heaven, or "Great Lodge above," is not the dwelling place of God the Father and His Son, the Lord Jesus Christ. It's the local (cosmically speaking) headquarters for the Cosmic Brotherhood of the Great White Lodge of Freemasonry.

Alice tells us on page ninety-eight of this book that the lodge on Sirius gets its energy from a lodge in the Pleiades, a distant formation of seven stars. (Mayan, the girl friend of David—Shirley MacLaine's guru—was supposedly from the Pleiades.) Bailey enumerates for us some of the cosmic influences which, she says, affect the consciousness of men, especially during the process of initiation.

First and foremost is the energy or force emanating from the sun Sirius. If it might be so expressed, the energy of thought, or mind force, in its totality, reaches the solar system from a distant cosmic centre via Sirius. Sirius acts as the transmitter, or the focalizing centre, whence emanate those influences which produce self-consciousness in man. . . .

Another type of energy reaches man from the Pleiades, passing through the Venusian scheme to us, just as the Sirian energy passes through the Saturnian. . . . These facts involve the secrets of the mysteries. . . . (A. Bailey, *Initiation* 98-9)

She says if we but knew all the mysteries wrapped up in these facts, we'd understand the secrets of the universe: "In the mystery of this influence, and in the secret of the sun Sirius, are hidden the facts of our cosmic evolution, and incidentally, therefore, of the solar system." (A. Bailey, *Initiation*, 188)

I might add that in all this nonsense is revealed the fact of Freemasonry's close association and entanglement with these demons masquerading as "the Hierarchy" and foisting all this hocus-pocus on the millions of those in the New Age movement and the Eastern religions who sincerely believe this malarkey! But, read on! It gets more incredible the further we delve into the writings of the New Age queen and her husband, Foster!

Master Masons of the Universe

On page twenty-one of *The Spirit of Masonry*, Foster Bailey tells us about the "Master Masons of the Universe," who have watched over mankind's progress on the long road of evolution, and, he reveals, that's the story depicted in the first three degrees of Masonry.

Such, symbolically, is the progress and mode of achievement for every human soul; such has been the path trodden by all the Saviors of the race. From darkness to light all must go. . . . He must learn that the experience . . . is the only thing that can fit him to join the ranks of the Master Masons of the Universe, and carry on the eternal quest in company with all brothers.

This is the revelation which the passage of the candidate through all the degrees conveys. . . . Subtle and illusive indications are given also of that organized and intelligent activity which is carried on by that Grand Lodge of Master Masons who have for ages watched over humanity and guided men steadily in the way of light. . . . The whole fabric of Masonry may be regarded as the externalization of that inner spiritual group whose members, down the ages, have been custodians of the Plan. (F. Bailey, 21-2)

Next, he writes that these Master Masons are called by many names, such as "Christ and His church. . . . They can be known by others as the Masters of the Wisdom. . . , the Dispensers of Light." Then, he adds,

They are therefore sometimes known as the Illuminati. . . . They are the Rishis of the oriental philosophy, the builders of the occult tradition. . . . Stage by stage they assist at the unfolding of the consciousness of the candidate until the time comes when he can "enter into light" and, in his turn become a light-bearer, one of the Illuminati who can assist the Lodge on High in bringing humanity to light. (F. Bailey, 22-3)

As any Mason knows, "entering into light" is the term used in the fulfillment of his "search for light" in the degrees of Masonry. Bailey has just stated that this can make him one of the Illuminati—one of those "illumined" ones who can help the Masonic Grand Lodge on Sirius "bring humanity into light." (That is, bring them under demonic control.)

Foster Bailey says that participating in this great work as part of a greater initiation—the Luciferic Initiation that Creme says will take place in Masonic lodges—will take one on to his own godhood: "The rites, ceremonies and initiations of Masonry may be regarded (and are so regarded by many) as being faint representations and symbolic rehearsals of those major spiritual initiations through which every human being must pass before achieving his goal of manifested divinity and can enter finally within the veil."[13] So, we see that, like any good New Age occultist, a Mason's goal is to become a god, himself.

Evolution of the Races

Another revelation concerns the "evolution" of the races as given by Foster starting on page thirty-one and as explained more fully by H.P.B. and Alice in their works. Foster presents what he calls a basic hypothesis in discussing the question: "Is Masonry of vast antiquity and do we inherit it from a dim and distant past?"

That the hypothesis is far more than that for the New Agers is evident when later he says that if you can't accept this hypothesis, you just need to be more open to your intuition, a veiled reference to paying attention to the demons trying to influence you. Foster Bailey says the hypothesis, based on a study of the rituals and symbols and the allegory of initiation, is as follows:

> Masonry is the descendent of, or is founded upon, a divinely imparted religion which long antedates the prime date of creation as given in our Bible. [It] is all that remains to us of the first world religion which flourished in an antiquity so old that it is impossible to affix a date. It was the first unified world religion. Then came the era of separation of many religions, of sectarianism. Today we are working again towards a universal world religion. Again then, Masonry will come into its own, in some form or another. (F. Bailey, 30-1)

Bailey further says that this ancient religion is attested to by "such symbols as the pyramids, both in Egypt and South America. . . , what is left to us of the ancient mysteries."[14] He says these mysteries "were temporary custodians of the ancient truth and [are] closely allied to the Masonic work of today . . . and the golden thread of the living continuity can be traced through them to modern Masonry."[15]

Bailey then says that we can go even further back than that in our search for the source of the Masonic inheritance.

> Masonry may therefore be as old as humanity itself, and religion as old as Masonry. . . , the period

when there emerged on earth that infant humanity of which our modern race of men are the fruit-
age. That period may also have been the founding
of. . . . our Masonic ritual and work. . . .

Scientists hint at two races which preceded ours
and give them names—The Lemurian civilization
and the Atlantean civilization. Ancient Lemuria
saw the first human being walk on the earth. He
was little more than an animal. (F. Bailey, 35)

Then Foster makes a statement about this prehuman
creature that should set every Mason bolt upright in his
chair.

He was a soul in a deep and dark prison with the
light that is hidden in each human form lost and
veiled. . . . He was a poor blind candidate for light,
knocking blindly upon the door of the Temple.
Blind and ignorant he wanders up and down, seeking light and unable to answer the questions put
to him. (F. Bailey, 35-6)

So, we see that Bailey says this prehuman creature
was "a poor blind candidate for light, knocking blindly
upon the door of the Temple." That is a verbatim description of the initiate during the ceremony of the first degree of Masonry! But, for those of you who are not Masons, you need not take my word for it because, in the
next sentence, Foster, himself, says that's what it represents:

"This is beautifully taught in the E.A. [Entered Ap-
prentice] initiation where all he can do, until the gift of
light is conferred upon him, is to express his willingness
to seek. Every other question, when put to him, is answered by his escort."[16]

We can now better understand what Albert Mackey
meant by his description of the symbology of the First
Degree. Writing in his *Encyclopedia of Freemasonry*, he states:
"The Entered Apprentice Degree symbolizes the creation
of man and his first perception of light."[17]

Let's continue with the thread of the true meaning of

the Blue Lodge initiations as Foster now proceeds to show that not only the First Degree has as its purpose to recount that time in prehistory when animal-man became man, but that the second and third degrees also tell part of this story.

> Later the Atlantean civilization succeeds and the race of men reach a point where they can begin to "subdue their passions" and cultivate those arts and sciences which will raise them up into a higher scale of living. . . . This is the lesson of the F.C. [Fellow Craft, or Second] initiation.
>
> Today in our Aryan race, humanity . . . is now ready for a further revelation. He can be permitted to take the sublime degree of M.M. [Master Mason] and receive the Master's Word for which he so long has sought. . . . All this racial history is indicated in the work of the three degrees of the Blue Lodge . . . and the rhythm of the threefold work of the Past, the Present and Future lies revealed. (F. Bailey, 36)

If you are a Mason, I suggest you reread the previous pages and consider how those you trusted in Masonry have lied to you from the start about the real meaning of what your initiation signified. If you were also a Christian at this time, whose Lord is the Light of the World, and "in Whom there is no darkness," can you really accept the description of your state as an Entered Apprentice as one who was in darkness, a poor, blind soul searching for light?

So, there you have it. Masonry, say the New Agers, is the original religion of not only the world, but also of that part of the universe ruled by Lucifer, and it's a worship carried out in the Grand Lodge on Sirius as well as in Masonic lodges everywhere else.

Masonic "Group Work" Is Magic

Earlier, we read of Masonry's true "work" as being witchcraft and magic. Foster Bailey also discusses this

aspect of Masonry in his book *The Spirit of Masonry*. He
says that "even the most advanced esotericists in the fraternity" are even yet only dimly aware of the true "creative" nature of the Masonic work. He likens this creative
work to that which God did when he spoke into existence
the worlds through "the Word as a creating factor." He
says,

> The Hindu expresses it thus: "God thought. God
> visualized. God spoke. The worlds came into be-
> ing." Behind the constitution of a Lodge lies this
> basic truth, and the work of a Lodge, through its
> rituals and ceremonies, is intended to be a train-
> ing school for creative work.[18]

This creative work is accomplished when "a Lodge of
Masons" becomes unified and is enabled "to work together as one functioning coherent body." The Masons
learn by "participating in such a ritual, to work, say and
think the same thing simultaneously."[19]

We've already quoted parts of this earlier in another
context. But, here let us point out that anyone the least
bit familiar with magic and witchcraft will recognize this
as a description of a witches' coven carrying out their
"work," which is called "creative work."

Bailey emphasizes the need for "a formulated uniformity of thought" so that every move, every action "may
have behind it, and underlying it, the concentrated attention and thought power of the assembled Masons." The
power of this united thought "would be hypnotic in its
potency. . . . Masonry in its true and highest sense is
magical work."[20]

On the next page, he amplifies this "magical work."
He says a lodge of Masons will then "work" as a group for
humanity as a whole.

> They will create a focal point for spiritual light,
> and will organize themselves into a body of con-
> scious custodians of the mysteries, acting as a dis-
> tributing agency for knowledge. . . . The effective-
> ness of this possible work will be paralleled by the

increasing sensitivity of the race to telepathic impression. . . . They will consciously co-operate with the Lodge on High. . . . They will act as a dedicated lens through which the light can shine in the darkness . . . and the mysteries of initiation will no longer be only symbolic, but will constitute a definite form of activity, carried forward upon earth. (F. Bailey, 98)

Bailey states that this cooperation with the Lodge on High "will blend the minds of many into one directed purpose" and will help empower the candidates for initiation to meet the tests of that initiation. Then, he states, "Behind the magical work of the rituals must be the influence of the established rhythm. . . . The materializing upon earth of the mystical vision . . . must be brought about by the wise working of this law of rhythm and of ritual."[21]

Alice A. Bailey's many New Age books also give us a key to understanding more about this group work, which is directed by the demons in the heavenlies pretending to be "Masters of Wisdom" on Shambala. In *The Rays and the Initiations*, she states, "The group can be, and frequently is, responsive to the 'bright centre,' Shambala. . . . Here is the clue to the significance of group work. One of its major functions, esoterically speaking, is to absorb, share, circulate, and then distribute energy."[22] She also discusses the "need for telepathic sensitivity in every group composed of disciples. . . . The cultivation of an inter-relation of a telepathic nature upon the mental plane is essential."[23]

The demon spirit calling himself the Tibetan, Djwhal Khul, speaking through her, emphasizes the importance of this witchcraft, or group work, in "thought formulation and thought-form creation." He says,

Then a clear thought-form can be constructed with definiteness and it can be positively directed. . . , working on mental levels with your group brothers so that your thought-form is a part of their thought-form and you can, therefore, unitedly

produce a living, embodied form which can be
directed as I may determine.(A. Bailey, *Discipleship in the New Age*, [New York, 1944] 1:65)

The capability for this group work is not yet here, at
least back when these words were written, but it will
become available to the Hierarchy, we are promised, when
the brothers have been better prepared for its rigors of
concentrated, purposeful thought and visualization. In
the meantime, we are told, "the spiritual thought, result-
ing in magical work of one brother of pure intent, is of
far greater potency than that of many brothers who follow the tendencies of the personality."[24]

And, what are the requirements for a brother to be
able to take part in this witchcraft? Bailey says, "The white
magician is he who utilizes all power and knowledge in
the service of the race. . . , the technique of the Great
Work. . . . The white magician works with the forces of
nature and swings them back into control of advanced
humanity."[25] The goal of this group work is to hasten the
materializing on earth of the Hierarchy, heralded by the
return of "the Christ."

Externalization of the Hierarchy
Brings the Anti-Christ

This New Age Christ is not Jesus Christ of the Christians. The Master Jesus is, New Agers say, simply a lower
level initiate. But, the purpose of the New Age is to bring
in a one-world religion and government headed by "The
Christ, the Lord Maitraya," who is the Fifth Buddha, and
this will bring into physical incarnation the Hierarchy,
itself, as Alice Bailey explains in *The Rays and the Initiations*: "The externalization of the Hierarchy, therefore,
and the restoration of the Mysteries, . . . are an expression of the inherent spiritual impulse. . . . The Hierarchy
has its own life, and its own goals and objectives [which]
will become more familiar to thinking men as the Hierarchy approaches closer to the physical plane."[26]

In *The Externalization of the Hierarchy*, Bailey tells us in
terms so clear even a novice Christian can understand

that what we're reading about in these New Age books are the battle plans of Satan's kingdom:

> The senior Members of the Hierarchy will not at first be the ones who will make the needed approach. Under Their direction and Their close supervision, this approach will be made—in the early stages—by initiates . . . and also by those disciples who will . . . work under their direction. It is only in the later stages, and when the time has come for the return into recognized physical expression of the Christ, leading to the definite restoration of the Mysteries that certain of the senior members of the Hierarchy will appear and take outer and recognizable physical control of world affairs. (A. Bailey, 570)

This is such a clear statement of the anti-Christ setting up his one-world government and universal one-world religion, based on the mystery religion of ancient Babylon, even someone with only a sketchy notion of Revelation should be able to discern that the New Age movement is Satan's plan to bring about the reign of the anti-Christ over the earth. In this same book, Bailey states that this takeover will have among its goals:

> 1. Creating and vitalizing the new world religion. 2. The gradual reorganizing of the social order. . . . 3. The public inauguration of the system of initiation. This will involve the growth and comprehension of symbolism. 4. The esoteric training of disciples and of humanity in this new cycle. (A. Bailey, *Externalization of the Hierarchy*, 700)

In *Esoteric Psychology II*, she sheds more light on this event.

> Another important objective of the Plan . . . is the emergence into physical plane activity, of the group of souls of Whom the New Group of world Servers are the outer representatives. This appearance can be called (in Christian phraseology) the sec-

ond coming of Christ with His Disciples, or it can
be called the manifestation of the planetary Hierarchy, or the appearance of the Masters of the
Wisdom, Who will restore upon earth the ancient
mysteries and institute again the order of Initiation." (A. Bailey, *Esoteric Psychology II* [New York:
Lucis Publishing Co., 1980], 649)

Masonry Is the Core of the New Age World Religion

Alice Bailey finally gives away the big secret:

[T]he Christ and the Masters are occupied with
the task of preparing for the restoration of the
Mysteries. This restoration will fall into three phases
and will cover and include in its symbolism all
phases of human unfoldment. The story of mankind will be pictorialized. These three phases correspond broadly and in a general sense to the
three degrees of the Blue Lodge in Masonry. The
analogy is not entirely accurate, owing to the un-
avoidable degeneracy of Masonry, but with the
restoration of the Mysteries, Masonry will come
into its own. . . . [The ritual of the Master Mason
Degree] will be objectively staged and the general
public will recognize it as the major rite and ritual
of the new religious institution of the period. This
is the stage where the forces of resurrection are
active, when the Lord is with His people and the
Christ has returned to earth. (Alice A. Bailey,
Externalization, 574–5.)

There you have it. I don't know how it could be any
clearer. We've looked in detail at the mystery religions of
ancient days. We've heard from the top Masonic authorities and the top New Age authorities, who have agreed
that Freemasonry is the repository of the mysteries and
that a New Age world religion is being forged based on
these mysteries.

Now we've heard the direct statement from Alice Bailey/Djwahl Khul that the Blue Lodge degrees will form the heart of this new religion and that the mystery play of the third degree will be staged as its "major rite and ritual."

So, we see that Freemasonry is more than just the heart or core of the anti-Christ's New Age world religion—Freemasonry *is* the New Age world religion!

Endnotes

1. Albert Pike, *Morals and Dogma* (Richmond: L. H. Jenkins, Inc., 1924), 213.

2. *The Holy Bible* (Philadelphia: A. J. Holman Co., 1962).

3. Pike, 840.

4. Ibid., 731.

5. Ibid., 732.

6. Kent Philpott, *A Manual of Demonology and the Occult* (Grand Rapids, Michigan: Zondervan, 1976), 160.

7. Ibid., 163.

8. Benjamin Creme, *The Reappearance of the Christ and the Masters of Wisdom* (London: The Tara Press, 1980), 84.

9. Ibid., 86.

10. David Spangler, *Reflections of the Christ* (Scotland: Findhorn, 1977), 40-4.

11. Ibid.

12. A. Bailey, *Discipleship in the New Age* (New York, 1955), 2:15-6.

13. F. Bailey, *The Spirit of Masonry* (Kent, England: Lucis Press Ltd., 1957), 23.

14. Ibid., 32.

15. Ibid.

16. Ibid., 35-6.

17. Albert Mackey, *Encyclopedia of Freemasonry* (Chicago, New York, London: The Masonic History Co., 1924), 14.

18. F. Bailey, *Spirit*, 95-6.

19. Ibid.

20. Ibid., 97.

21. Ibid., 99.

22. A. Bailey, *The Rays and the Initiations*, In *Serving Humanity*, (New York: Lucis Publishing Co., 1977), 68.

23. A. Bailey, *Discipleship* Vol. 2, 63.

24. A. Bailey, *A Treatise on White Magic*, In *Serving Humanity*, (New York: Lucis Publishing Co., 1977), 460.

25. A. Bailey, *Esoteric Psychology I* (New York: Lucis Publishing Co., 1967), 359.

26. A. Bailey, *Rays* (New York: Lucis Publishing Co., 1971), 333-5.

Four

Mixing Oil with Water

Rev. Harmon Taylor
(taken from a sermon)

I'm going to share something with you I have entitled "Mixing Oil with Water." You'll quickly understand the subject; we'll be using the Word of God and many selected Scripture portions at the very beginning of this message. This is the message on Freemasonry that I presented to the United Methodist church I pastored on my way out of the pastoral ministry.

Charles G. Finney was one of the foremost preachers of his day. He was a theologian who accepted Christ in 1821 and served Him until his death in 1875. He fulfilled the pastoral role in several churches. He became one of the most renown professors of systematic theology in all of history. But most of all he served his Lord to the very best he knew how to do, and that's what I'm trying to do.

Finney said when faced with a challenge you should do this: study it in the light of Scripture and act upon it in the light of Scripture. "Every local branch of the Church of Christ is bound to examine this subject and pronounce upon this institution according to the best light they can get."

I have been involved in Freemasonry; I have been involved in the church as a believer and as a pastor; I have been a pastor and teacher. I have been involved in the reading of His Word, and I have been involved in the comparison of the Word of God as I see it in Holy Scripture versus the Word of God as it is given me in the ritual of the Masonic Fraternity. Invariably, words are changed. So, let us look at mixing oil with water.

Let me share from Psalm 118:22: "The stone, the very stone which the builder rejected, it has become the capstone. The Lord has done this, it is a marvelous thing in our eyes. This is the day which the Lord has made, let us rejoice and be glad in it." Then, moving over to Matthew 5:33-37, Jesus is speaking about perjury and retaliation being forbidden.

> Again you have heard that it was said to the people long ago, do not break your oath, but keep your oaths you have made to the Lord. But I tell you, says Jesus, do not swear at all, Either by heaven, for it is Gods' throne, or by the earth for it is His footstool, or by Jerusalem for it is the city of the great king, and do not swear by your head, for you cannot make even one hair either white or black, simply let your yes be yes and your no be no. Anything beyond that comes from the evil one.

These are not my words now; these are the words of Jesus. And, then moving over to Matthew 24:1-2: "Jesus left the temple and was walking away when His disciples came to Him to call attention to its buildings. Do you see all these things? Jesus asked. I tell you the truth, not one stone here will be left on another. Every one of them will be thrown down."

Then, moving over to 2 Timothy 3:16, 17: "All Scripture is God-breathed and useful for teaching, for rebuking, for correcting, and for training in righteousness, so that the man of God may be thoroughly equipped for every good work."

Second Timothy chapter four, words the Lord has laid upon my heart, has been reinforced so many times. Before I ever spoke them as a section of Scripture that the Lord was dealing with me on, my daughter placed that Scripture in my hand. Just the lettering, 2 Timothy 4:2–5: This was Paul's message to Timothy, a pastor. And, it is a message to every pastor; it is a message that certainly God had for this pastor. He has burned it into my heart:

> Preach the Word. Be prepared in season and out of season, correct, rebuke and encourage with great patience and careful instructions for the time will come when men will not put up with sound doctrine, instead, to suit their own desires they will gather around them a great number of teachers to say what their itching ears want to hear. They will turn their ears away from the truth and turn aside to myths. But you, keep your head in all situations, endure hardship, do the work of an Evangelist, discharge the duties of your ministry.

That is God's call upon me and that is what I am trying to do. Another Scripture verse relating back to Matthew 5 is James 5:12, which says, "Above all my brothers, do not swear. Not by heaven, nor by earth, nor by anything else. Let your yes, be yes and your no, no—or you will be condemned."

God have mercy on us as we share together around these Scripture verses. I had been pastor of my church for a little more than a year. God had been moving dramatically in my life. He moved dramatically just to bring me to Clifton Park United Methodist Church. We worked together as a pastor and people, and in that time, one word had stood out above all others in my Christian walk, and it is this: Be careful, Pastor, of deception. As God moved in my life in those months, I had been able to see how easy it was for me and for others to be deceived and drawn away from the Christian walk. It was in October of the same year that I shared with them the dark roots of Halloween and how it was brought into sync with the Christian holiday of All Saints' Day.

I shared with them the evil of that; some rebuked it, but it is the call of a pastor to preach God's Word. Some of them learned, some of them were surprised. I was even more surprised when a brother in Christ came to me. He had been praying for four months—remember Nehemiah? This brother prayed for four months before he came to me to talk about my involvement in a cult! "Bob, what are you talking about? Me? Involved in a cult? I'm in the United Methodist Church!" And, then we began to share together.

I realized that while I was sharing with the church that they needed to be careful about dabbling in the occult even if it were just the dressing in a costume, here I was in a full blown cult. It's not easy for me to share that with you, for what you might think, and how could I be so stupid. I've shared with others and actually had Christians laugh at me. Please, don't laugh. But, listen. As a pastor, as a preacher, as a child of the King, I must preach the Word without fear of man's criticism. I must preach it with the reverential fear of the love of God for the souls of all men.

Now, we will deal with a topic that may be uncomfortable to some of you. To others, it may tell you something you have already suspected. To others, it will confirm what you already knew. At the very start, I need to assure you that my object is not to attack or challenge any individual man, woman, or child. What I share with you has little to do with a man or woman or child, but it affects the lives of many men, women, and children. And, it is that evil that I speak against this day.

I am not attacking a person, but I am seeking to lead men and women into a closer walk with the one, true God—the Father of our Lord Jesus Christ. I do this in the name of Christ for the glory of God and hopefully with a boldness of a Charles G. Finney, a nineteenth century evangelist, who spoke as God gave him utterance.

First, let's look at the dictionary definition of *immoral*. Webster defines it as conflicting with generally and traditionally held moral principles. Concerning the fraternity of Freemasons, my Christian friends, their benevolence, their moral principles in general, Charles G. Finney accurately states the following:

> Masonry does not recognize the Bible as any higher authority with Masons than the sacred books of heathen nations nor the Koran of Mohammed or the Verti of Hindu. That Freemasonry recognizes all religions is equally valid. That so far as Masonry is concerned, it matters not at all what the religion of its adherents is, provided they are not Atheists.

To join the Masonic Fraternity, you need not be a Christian. I could ask you to raise your hands as to how many of you think that the Masonic Fraternity is a Christian organization, and, probably, one third of you would raise your hand until you think about it or remember that there are Jews and many others in that organization, and the reason for that is that it requires a belief in only one god. Any god! Just one.

I'm not the first to stand up and speak out against it. I'm just one of the latest. I'm going to share with you the names on a remarkable list of great Christian men and statesmen who renounce the lodges and opposed them, and this is particularly important to you if you happen to be upset because one of the most illustrious figures in religion to speak out against Masonry was a man by the name of John Wesley. Yes, I'm going back to Methodism, right back to the very root: that man who left his church and preached the salvation message to miners in England. Yes, John Wesley took a stand against Masonry.

Alexander Campbell, Daniel Webster, Wendell Phillips, Chief Justice Charles Marshall, Charles Summner, John Hancock, Horace Greeley, Dwight L. Moody, R. A. Tory, Timothy Dwight, Charles Finney, Charles Blanchard, John Adams, John Quincy Adams, John Madison, Amos Wells, Simon Peter Long, James M. Gray are all part of a long list of men who spoke out against Masonry. Listen to these powerful words of Dwight L. Moody to pastors.

I don't see how any Christian most of all a Christian Minister can go into these secret lodges with unbelievers. They say they have more influence for good but I say they can have more influence for good by staying out of them and then reproving their evil deeds. Abraham was more influence for good in Sodom than Lot was for good. True reformers separate themselves from the world rather than becoming a part of it. But Dwight L. Moody, some say, if you talk that way you'll drive out all the members of secret societies out of your meetings and out of your churches, "What if I did?" said Dwight L. Moody, better men will take their places. Give them the truth anyway and if they would rather leave their churches than their lodges the sooner they get out of the churches, the better. Those are the words of an Evangelist, a Prophet, Dwight L. Moody. "I would rather have ten members," he said, "who are separated from the world than a thousand such members. Come out of your lodges. Better be one with God than a thousand without Him."

Concerning a Christian as a member of a Masonic society, we have this from the very Word of God: "And I heard a voice from heaven saying 'Come out of her my people that Ye not be partakers of her sin and you receive not her plagues for her sins have reached unto heaven and God hath remembered her iniquities'" (Rev. 18:4–5).

There are many Christians, even ministers of the Gospel of Christ who support the adherence to the teachings of the Masonic lodge. I have been a Mason; I have been a Past Master of my lodge; I received the Master of the Year Award in my district for increasing the lodge attendance by 259 percent over the previous year. Yes, I was committed to it. I'm ashamed of it now. But, it took a lot of time from my church, from my family, from my sleep. I did the best job I knew how to do.

I was appointed a New York State Grand Chaplain; there's sixty-some in the state. I was one of them, and I was selected personally by the Grand Master because of my leadership and because of my service. Normally, it goes through a district committee where Right Worshipfuls get together, but they were saving me for District Deputy Grand Master.

The Grand Master personally appointed me to that post. I served him as best I could. But, what it says or should say to you is that I speak with the authority of the Word of God, and I speak with the full knowledge of the rituals. I have performed the degrees in the Blue Lodge. I have seen them all, observed, and been a part of them. There is a real question of what can be done with the great numbers of professed Christians, including Christian pastors who are in the Masonic Fraternity. But, I tell you, I pray for them every single day.

Let me just share with you what one pastor said. I wrote an editorial in the newspaper. All I did was commend my denomination in England and the Roman Catholic church for taking a stand against Masonry. In part, I said,

> I write as one who is well informed and not confused, and in no need of help concerning this matter. Stanley Maxwell was quoted as saying "The lodge honors Jesus Christ as it honors Socrates, Buddha, Mohammed." Christians and others need to know that Masonry honors none of these. They aren't mentioned in any form of honor in the Fraternity. Their names aren't mentioned and neither is the name of my Savior Jesus Christ. There is no place in ritual of the Masonic Fraternity where Jesus is acknowledged as "Your Savior."

What was the response by a man who was the chairman of a district board of ministry that I answered to, in order to stand in my pulpit: "a Grand Chaplain, Mr. Taylor has expressed his biased opinion, and his faith seems to have been adversely affected."

What men will do! What men will do in order to
protect their fraternity—even to the putting down of a
fellow pastor. Charles G. Finney was a Mason, came out
of it when he accepted Christ, and he wrote a whole book
on it. The air has almost been darkened by the immense
number of falsehoods that have been circulated by Freemasonry to destroy the reputation of every man who has
renounced Freemasonry.

Anybody come to you and criticized you? You know,
back home, somebody came into an insurance office and
told a member of my congregation, "It's a good thing you
got rid of that guy when you did." She said to him, "We
didn't get rid of him, we wanted to keep him. He left."

A week after I came out of the fraternity the man who
wrote the *History of Masonry* gathered together the officers of my former lodge, told them what a tragic loss it was
that I'd left. He reminded them about my year in a back
brace, told them that I'd been on some strong medication
and evidently it had affected my mind.

Well, I'll tell you what the medication was. It was two
Valium prescribed by the doctor while I was in the hospital for two weeks, reduced to half that amount when I
got out of the hospital, and that was two years before I
made the decision to leave Masonry. That medication is
awful slow working! I think any doctor would be able to
document that it didn't come from that medication. But,
hallelujah! He spoke to the Master of my lodge, and you
know what happened? A week after I left Masonry, he
signed my demit—before the next meeting. Let me share
it with you:

> To the Secretary;
> I am resigning as a member of Welcome Lodge
> 829. There is a better light, that light is the light
> of the Lord and Savior Jesus Christ. In His Word
> (Jn. 8:12) it says: I am the light of the world, who-
> ever follows me will not walk in darkness. I have
> walked in the darkness of Masonry. Today I am
> ending that darkness and following the One, True,
> Light, that of God, His Son, and The Holy Spirit.

Hallelujah! I did more for Jesus Christ by leaving Masonry than I ever did by being in it, and that's just the beginning. You know what else happened? The next day, his son left and gave his testimony! And, you know what else happened? That week they had a midweek prayer meeting in the church on Wednesday night.

I called up a man who walked by me one day at the Pine View Community Church, and he said to me, "I don't know how you could be a minister and a Mason." He was a wimpy kind of guy, so I just ignored it, but God didn't let me forget it. And, when I left the Fraternity, I called him on the phone and told him that I'd come out of Masonry, and he said "Oh, great! Can I use that as a testimony tonight at worship?" My gut reaction was to tell them myself, but I realized that that was my pride, so I agreed. He went to that prayer meeting, and he shared. There was a guy there with his Masonic bible with its big Masonic emblem on it. And, as he heard about this Mason writing a letter to the Grand Chaplain and leaving Masonry, he pulled the Bible closer to him. Next to him was a dear black lady who learned a long time ago how to really pray. It got to prayer time and she stood up and started to pray that God would use that letter to lead other men out of the Fraternity by the hundreds. He could take no more of it. He picked up his Bible and stormed out of the church. This fellow that I'd been talking to saw that Masonic emblem and he said, "I've offended that brother."

When I got home, there was a message from the Mason waiting. My wife knew I wouldn't be in until late, but he said, "Have him call me whatever time he gets in." I called him, it was after midnight, now in the morning of the next day, and he said, "I hear that you are Grand Chaplain and you got a letter from a guy that's leaving Masonry. Do you know anything about it?" I said, "Sure, I know all about it; I wrote the letter." He replied, "I gotta talk to you." And, so we went down, and we ate at the Hilton Hotel. We sat there, and we prayed, and he told me his testimony. He wanted to know how to get out and what to do. You know, in that week, eight men came out of the Fraternity, and every single one of them gave a witness to the Lord Jesus Christ—hallelujah!

What's happening is that people don't know. You know why the Masonic Fraternity is a secret organization? Because if they ever showed me that ritual before I went through the door of that lodge, I would have laughed. Then, I would have gone home.

I don't know how other men got into Masonry, but I'll tell you how I got in. I was a pastor to my people in Hagemon, and I slipped up bad. I let the men of my church lead me in an area where I should have been leading them. When I looked out in the congregation, there were Masonic lapel pins on all but one of the men in my congregation. I couldn't get a men's group started in my church, and now I know why: they were all involved in Masonry; they didn't have time for another meeting a week. Since I couldn't get them to join a group, I joined the one they had. I asked them, and they were thrilled. They were happy; their minister was going to join.

There was a lady in that church, Marion Campbell, who didn't like my involvement in Masonry. I didn't have to worry about that because every time she spoke up, these men put her down. When there were some tough times in the church, some of those Masons who disagreed with what I was saying supported me because I was a Mason. Now, that's not the reason to support your pastor. It's easy to get led in.

Finney challenged men like myself. "Let Christian men labor with these Masons, plead with them, and endeavor to make them see that it is to be their duty to abandon it." He continued, saying, "the morality inculcated by Masons is an exclusive, one-sided, selfish affair. In its best estate it is only partiality and doing in a very slovenly manner the work of a mutual insurance company."

You see, when you get involved in Masonry, if you're given a choice between giving help to a Mason and somebody else, you help that Mason first, even if the other one is in more need. Let no man deceive you by any means;

Masonry claims for itself the power to conduct its disciples to heaven. You do it by your good works, and if
you are good in your works, you will get there.

In many places in the ritual, it teaches the candidate
the observance of Masonic law, principles, and usages
that will secure for him his salvation. I put a lot of those
things in a corner. Have you ever done that in your
house? You put a lot of things in a corner, and the house
looks pretty neat? But, when you pull all that stuff out of
the corner, what a mess! That's what happened with me
and Masonry. I stuck the salvation by works in one corner. I stuck some Scripture that wasn't quite right in
another corner.

I met with the Christian brother who prayed for me
for four months without my even knowing it, and, even
though one of his prayer partners moved all the way to
Carolina, he called her every week to pray with her for
me. That's the kind of commitment that came to me by
a brother and a sister in Christ to lead me out of Masonry. That brother and that woman even came to my
son's graduation because they couldn't believe that a
Mason would be allowed in the Laudenville Community
Church pulpit. And, when we met five months later, he
gave me a copy of that church bulletin, where he had
written down what I said and put a little Masonic symbol
with a question mark wherever what I said didn't line up
with Masonic ritual. He spent a lot of time and a lot of
effort, and that's what I'm trying to do with others. I
prayed over this message for nearly four months now.

> Let no man deceive you for that day shall not
> come except there come a falling away, first of
> that man of sin be revealed, the son of perdition
> who opposeth and exhalteth himself above all that
> is called God, or that is worshipped, so that he as
> God sitteth in the temple of God showing himself
> that he is God. (2 Thess. 2:3-4)

Not only is Freemasonry a religion (it offers salvation
by works), but it also claims the position of God through

its very rituals. In the Seventh Degree of the Royal Arch Masons, there is a representative of the burning bush. I'll tell you how deep I got into this. I went through the Scottish Rite, the Fourth through the Thirty-second degree in Masonry. Some of you may know about the Thirty-second Degree of Masonry, and you think that it's a pretty good thing.

All it takes to be a Thirty-second Degree Mason, in Albany, is $135 and all day Saturday watching six plays performed in which you may be selected to participate in one. That's all it takes. But, praise a man for being a Thirty-second Degree Mason, and he's not going to tell you that. I never told anybody that when I was a Mason. The Seventh Degree of Royal Arch Masons has a representation of the burning bush. The candidate is told to take off his shoes, for the place where he stands is holy ground. And, then, the Master of the lodge claims to be the God of Abraham, Isaac, and Jacob. What an awful, profane, blasphemous thing this is!

It is my most sincere prayer that you will receive in a spirit of love and compassion what I endeavor to convince you of concerning the dangers of the Masonic Fraternity. I've been there! And, I'll tell you, it is only by the grace of God that I am out of there today!

Have you ever heard the story of the frog in the water? The frog sits in a pan of water very contentedly. You put the pan on a hot plate and begin to turn up the temperature very slowly, and the frog sits there very contentedly—as the temperature rises from 68 to 75 to 80 to 100 to 140 to 180 to 212. That frog will never jump out of that water. And, that's the way it is with Christians—when they get involved with the wrong things, just a little bit at a time. Then, you can get in, and when the water is boiling, you are still there. In my First Degree, I wanted out and, I knew why I wanted out. Yet, within four years, I was doing that degree and bringing other men into Masonry.

I was the frog in that story, but God kissed me with His Word, and now I am a child of the King! Does that make me a prince?

I am not trying to have any quarrel or controversy with any man, woman, or child who happens to be involved in Masonry. I am not disregarding the sensibility of any Mason regarding their pet institution. I do not want to assail them. I only want to point out that there come times in the church when we have the sacrament of Holy Communion, and you will find that if Masons have a conflict, they don't come to Holy Communion, they go to their lodge meeting.

What I wish to do is to stop the spread of this great evil in the Church of Jesus Christ! I wish to give you some information that brings light and life.

Do you know that in spite of the two editorials I had put in the newspaper about Freemasonry, not one member of my church came to me and asked me about Freemasonry? They went to somebody else who knows nothing and asked, "What do you think about that?" Or, they went to another Mason and they asked, "What do you think about that?"—a Mason to a Mason. No man came to me, nor woman, and asked me, "Why did you say that?" If you've got a question, go to your pastor and ask him!

What I wish to do is to stop the spread of this great evil in our church—in the whole Church. I wish to arouse young men who are Masons to understand the horrible consequences of their dealings in these solemn oaths. I wish to arouse young men who are not Freemasons to look before they leap. The Church and the Christians have been remiss in suffering a whole generation, including me, to grow up in ignorance of the character of Freemasonry. No minister ever told me about that. Not one denominational leader quietly gave me a single word of advice or warning.

In the 1800s, Masonry was exposed, and Masons abandoned their lodges for the shame of it. It cost one man, William Morgan, his very life. But, for me to lay down my life is gain; that holds no threat to me. This man wrote all of the rituals of Masonry in a book. The Masons kidnapped him from Batavia, New York, then they moved him out to Niagara, stored him in Ft. Niagara for three days, and then they took him out in a boat. They tied a rope—the Masons would call it a cabletow—around his waist (not quite Masonically) with a weight on it, and gave him one half hour to make his peace with his God. Even though he pleaded that he might be spared so that he might be able to care for his wife and his children, they killed him anyway. These aren't rumors. This is the death-bed testimony of a man named Henry Vallance, the man who pushed William Morgan off the bow of that boat.

In Masonic history, they call that event "the Morgan excitement." They said if he were a drinking man, he'd be a drunk. They try to defame and disgrace everybody who doesn't agree with them. Oh! And the theme of Masonry is tolerance! We must tolerate one another. They told me, "Ah, dear brother, you know when you say that prayer as Grand Chaplain, you can't end it in the name of Jesus because you might offend the Jewish brother." Where is the Masons' tolerance? Where's their tolerance to the fact that the Scripture tells us that we come to God the Father through Christ, His Son. They were telling me to pray an empty prayer! And, I remember saying to the Jewish brother—who was eating his ham dinner at the time and who told me not to pray in Jesus' name—that I would pray in Jesus' name and that when he heard the brief silence after my prayer before I said "Amen," that he could rest assured that I was saying, under my breath, "in Jesus' name."

Isn't that awful? See how far and how hot they had gotten the water around the frog! I had to say the name of Jesus under my breath. Well, I'm not saying it under my breath any more: Jesus Christ is my Savior and I'm serving Him! That's why I'm sharing with you! Masonry claims the souls of men.

Let me go back and tell you a little bit more about Henry Vallance. He was never arrested, and never tried for the crime—and in that you find something about Ma-sonry. The justices and law enforcement officials took great pains to conceal and to deceive, themselves. John

Quincy Adams was president of the United States of America at the time, and he gave a scathing attack against Masonry when he investigated the events behind it after leaving the presidency.

The Masons even established two false editions of Morgan's book. They circulated the false editions and brought them to Masons who had never read the true book and said, "Why, these rituals aren't correct!" Then, these Masons would become the spokesmen to prove that the Morgan book was a lie.

Charles G. Finney, had a copy of the real book, as he wrote his book. The Masons could now rightly claim that the book was not correct, but they did not have all the information. They'd been deceived by their own brothers.

The good news was that following that incident, forty-five thousand of the fifty thousand Masons in this country left their lodges. While Christians have slept, the fraternity has once again reared its ugly head and taken unto itself Christians and ministers of the gospel.

Now, how is the public to know what Freemasonry is? How are you to know? First, negatively, you are not going to find out what it is by reading most of the books written by Masons because they are not going to tell you the truth. They are not going to tell you their ritual or the real history of their ritual. Secondly, you cannot learn about Masonry from the oral testimony of Masons. They'll tell you anything but the truth because they need to protect that secret of their society. And thirdly, Masons who are under an oath not to reveal any of its secrets will not reveal them. Their testimony, therefore, cannot be trusted and is of no value on the subject of Freemasonry.

How, then, are you positively to know about Masonry? You can learn it from the published and oral testimonies of those who have taken the degrees, such as myself, and have afterwards renounced them and confessed the error and publicly renounced Masonry. You can know from these renouncing Masons that they are competent and credible witnesses for when they speak, they testify against themselves. Anyone who testifies against himself does not do it lightly. It is given with a certainty of incurring an unrelenting persecution. Now, you may ask, what have Masons said about me since I have left the fraternity? Yes, they will trample over a man or woman of God to defend their institution.

But, the Lord brings His justice to bear. I already mentioned the brother who said I was on drugs; what I didn't tell you is that the police came to this same brother's own door one night. They arrested his son—also a Mason—for peddling drugs. The Masons got together and got him completely off the hook, and he is still a member of the Masonic lodge! It's also noteworthy to mention a Thirty-third Degree Mason in Schenectady, New York, who spent two months in jail, while the Masons looked for a Masonic judge to get him off—and then all the records were done away with. He forged money orders and bounced checks on closed accounts! He's still a Mason today. You see, Masons are bound to do more than help a brother; they're to help a brother in distress, and it doesn't say what kind of distress.

A Mason may need a little bit of money and need some food, or it could be that he's committed a crime. It really makes no difference. And, as you get higher up in the degrees, even treason is covered over by the brethren. That means if you're a Mason and a policeman, and if you abide by the oath of the fraternity, and you're told to go and arrest another Mason, you call him on the phone and tell him to get out of town before you get to his door. It means that if you're mugged and go before the court and your lawyer is a Mason, and if the accused gives the Grand Masonic Hailing Sign of Distress, your lawyer is under oath to flaw your case so that the brother goes free. If you find a Mason on a jury and that Grand Masonic Hailing Sign is given, you are going to have a hung jury if that Mason carries out his oath, and many do! Adhering Masons have persecuted, and still do persecute, those who reveal their secrets, just as far as they dare.

Dear Christian friends, I submit to you that this is the

highest degree of intolerance! Witnesses who testify under such circumstances as I have been under are entitled to credit—especially as they could have had no conceivable motive for deceiving the public.

Look at the First Degree for a moment. I went to that Masonic lodge room dressed in a business suit. Members of my church were there! Masons! They went into the lodge room, and I was told to go into the other room. I went in there, and, they closed the door. They told me to take off all my clothes and put on a cape and pair of pants that was missing one leg. One brother stayed there; I didn't even know that man's name! He was in this small room with me, and then, he blindfolded me and put a cabletow, a rope, around my neck. Then, he knocked on the door. When asked who was there, the man said that I was a poor, blind, candidate desirous of having and receiving a part in the rites, light, and benefit of this lodge.

Masons ought to pay attention to the ritual that comes afterwards because I never did. I knew it, I learned it, I memorized it, but I didn't know what it meant. As I came through the door of that lodge, the Masons were saying that I, a born-again Christian pastor, was spiritually blind, and they say that about every Christian coming through the door of that lodge. They are not referring to the blindfold. The Masons sit on the sidelines when new members come in; the blindfold is on, so the Masons assume that the ritual refers to physical blindness. But the ritual, the words themselves, are talking about spiritual blindness.

I was led to the back of the lodge room, blindfolded and cabletowed, where the senior deacon told me that he was about to apply a sharp instrument to my naked right breast. I was waiting to get shot with a needle, or feel a knife, but in a split second that felt like an eternity, I felt the point of a compass, the kind you make circles with. And then they lead me on and I was scared! They told me to kneel for the benefit of prayer, and they said a prayer, a godless prayer, and then they asked me in whom I put my trust.

I wanted to run out of the lodge, but I didn't know where the door was because they had moved me around a couple of times, and I was blindfolded. I told them the only thing I could—that my trust is in God. They replied that my trust being in God was well-founded. Then, they told me to rise, follow my conductor, and fear no danger.

Whew! That felt good! But, you know what that was? That was the lamb being led to the slaughter.

I went from there and followed the rest of the ritual very comfortably. A member of my church escorted me through this, and I was brought up to the altar and told to kneel. I was told just how to place my hand on the Bible, God's Holy Word, and the oath began. They asked me, "Are you still willing to take the obligations? Say 'aye.' " I did. "Pronounce your name in full." I did. "And repeat after me, 'In the presence of Almighty God, in this worshipful lodge, of Entered Apprentice . . .' " I found myself saying, "I do promise and swear that I won't reveal the secrets, that I will help aid and assist a brother. . . ."

Remember, every person who is a Mason has done this—every single one. It's only the First Degree. This pastor did it, too, but God forgave me. Hand on the Bible, Masons say the words, "under the ancient penalty having my throat cut across, my tongue torn out and buried in the sand of the sea where the tide ebbs and flows twice in twenty-four hours, if I ever reveal the secrets of this lodge." I have secrets greater than that and I want to make them known!

Jesus Christ is Lord, and I'm not bound by any oath that is in violation of His law, and His law says let your yes be yes and do not take any oath lest you come under condemnation! Now, I really don't care if Masons get upset by that, as long as my God does not condemn me. And, every Mason ought to know that, too.

In the Third Degree, the candidate's hands are placed on the Bible, "binding myself under no less a penalty than having my body severed in twain, my bowels taken thence and burned to ashes and scattered to the four winds of heaven that there might not remain tract, trace, or remembrance of so vile and perfect a wretch if I should violate this, my obligation." Would you let me pastor in your church if you knew I took that oath? Only the Masons would have. God forgive me; and He has. That's why I speak out! And, you can find out and verify everything I'm saying. You think its a secret society? In your local library, you can get the ritual book; you can get the information about Masonry. Also, there are numerous books now available in almost every Christian bookstore.

Do you still think Freemasonry is a Christian institution? Do you really think a pastor ought to be involved in it? Are you going to be proud to tell others that your pastor is a Mason? Or, are you going to be proud to tell them that he got out?

Dear Mason, are you proud to be a Mason now, during the daylight hours, as you consider the rituals you've taken part in? The Junior Warden says that he observes the Summit Meridian. That's sun worship. The Senior Warden observes the sun as it sets in the West at the close of day, and the Worshipful Master observes the sun in the East. There are three candles around the altar, one for the Master of the lodge, one for the sun god, and one for the moon god!

Also, one of the passwords to get into one of the York Rite bodies is "I am that I am!" "I am" is Jesus Christ Himself! Furthermore, in the Knights' Templar degree, the lodge has a Bible on the altar, a skull on top of that, and wine in the skull, and the Masons take a sip. Only one person does this for everybody. He takes a sip of the wine, and then agrees that if he violates that obligation, not only his sins but the sins of the person whose brain resided in the skull and the sins of Judas Iscariot would be upon him. No Christian should ever be a Mason!

I just want to deal with one Scripture, the prayer of the Chaplain. In the Masonic ritual, the Chaplain's prayer says, "Most Holy and Glorious Lord God, Great Architect of the Universe, Thou hast promised where two or three are gathered in Thy name, Thou wilt be in the midst." Does that sound scriptural to you? Well, almost. The

Scripture is, "Where two or three are gathered in my name, I will be in their midst." The difference is their "Thy" refers to the Masonic god, *jahbulon*. In the real Scripture, the "my" refers to Jesus Christ! There's the big difference. You see, the name of Jesus can't be mentioned in the lodge room—not even by a Grand Chaplain to end his prayer.

Dear Christian, if you're a Mason, I plead with you to hear my words. Run from Freemasonry to save your own soul. And women, if you're in a Masonic-related body, the Amaranth, the Eastern Star, the White Shrine, run from them! The base and the foundation of Masonry is rotten. You don't want to be on the fourteenth floor of a building with a crumbling foundation, do you? Well, let me tell you, its not just the foundation that's crumbling, the structure is too.

The Eastern Star symbol is the inverted five-pointed star. Let me tell you about this star. One of the founders of the Eastern Star, the man who wrote all the ritual, Rob Morris, chose that five-pointed star. He selected it for a specific reason out of mythology: it is the Goat of Mendes! And, ladies, did you know that the Goat of Mendes is the god of lust? How blasphemous that Morris would choose for his wife and his children a symbol of the Goat of Mendes, the god of lust.

Well, they don't think of it that way. An extended debate in Michigan yielded this result on whether or not to change the symbol: "This emblem, which has been our symbol, although evil, has been redeemed by the good works of its members." "This symbol, although evil"—who said it was evil? The Grand Chapter of the state of Michigan admitted it! "Has been redeemed by the good works of its members"—biblical salvation is through Christ alone, never by good works!

If you're a Mason, I urge you to flee from that Masonic altar. If you are in the Eastern Star or the Amaranth, please leave. Don't stay for a friend; don't stay for a relative. Don't stay for a Masonic funeral. Continuance in this cultic, demonic diversion from the Christian walk will sentence you to hell! That's according to God's Word, not mine. You may not have another day.

If you're not in, stay out! You see, salvation is not by works as Masons claim. Salvation is only by God's grace through Jesus Christ and His shed blood. And, if you don't believe that, you're not a Christian! And, if you do believe it, you should not be a Mason!

I really thank you for taking the time and for letting me unburden my heart on this subject—to let you know why I came out of Masonry. I hope you understand the love and concern that compelled me to do that. Yes, even at the risk of my very life.

When I came out of Masonry, I called my son as he got home from school and told him that I'd left the Masonic Fraternity. It was just one year after I was elected Grand Chaplain, and he stood in the highest place of honor and placed on my neck the Grand Chaplains' jewel. He said, "Dad, I've been praying for that for two years." A son of mine had been praying that I'd come out of Masonry! He even had a videotape to explain Masonry in the house! But, because it wasn't the right time, he let it go.

I also called my daughter and told her that night that I came out of Masonry. She said, "I'm glad, Dad. Praise The Lord! I've been praying for that for four years!" I didn't come out easy. But, I came out with a lot of friends!

Dear Christian friends, don't be upset if a member of your family is in Masonry. You pray. If you're a Mason, hear my words and come out, so the people don't have to continue to pray for you, year after year! And, the people of God said, "Amen!"

Five

Freemasonry Around the World

Mick Oxley

Mick Oxley is a retired wing commander for the Royal Air Force Commander and a transplant from the United Kingdom. Mick spent much of his service time in the Middle East, where he converted to the Islamic faith and searched deeply into Eastern Mysticism. Also heavily involved with Masonry, it would seem that Mick was lost to God forever. But, praise God! His sure Word says that He will save us, even from the "Uttermost." Today, Mick and his wife, Betty, serve the risen Savior, Jesus Christ. They live near Crescent City, Florida and are proud to be American citizens. Mick is a very much sought-after speaker for churches and conferences.

Ten years ago, you would have found very few Christian books written on Freemasonry. Today, it seems we have more books on Freemasonry than we have versions of the Bible. I seem to spend quite a lot of time answering letters and telephone messages, however well intentioned, by people who want me to read their script or book they feel compelled to write on Freemasonry. Only a few months ago, I had a letter from a chap in Sweden who wanted information so he could write a book on Masonry. He had gotten my name from Bill Schnoebelen's book *Masonry, Beyond the Light*.

I wrote back straight away, advising him that it would be far better for him to translate Bill's book into Swedish, as I said Bill's book is one of the best in the world exposing Freemasonry.

Most of the scripts and new books I have seen are pretty good, but a rare few of them come out with the truth of Freemasonry and its Luciferian doctrine and worship. I have to say that I am not surprised. The ignorance of things Satanic, of spiritual warfare in the Church, is devastating because it is doing exactly that to the Church—devastating it. I point the finger at the pulpits and blame the seminaries. But, with a Bible in your hand daily, getting into the Word of God, it is all there, and there is no excuse.

You will never fully understand Freemasonry unless you fully understand the teachings of the Bible on the things of the spirit. I am not here to lecture you, but I pray that, upon leaving here, you will have learned more of the power behind this occult organization and equally important, the power Jesus Christ has given us to come against the powers of darkness.

The Bible has to be our standard. While we can quote Pike, Hall, and Mackey until the cows come home, we cannot fight against the spirit world, teach on it, or write about it, unless we apply the Bible teaching, thus obtaining this vast knowledge of spiritual warfare. And, this, dear friends, is what the battle against Freemasonry is all about. As Paul says, "He who is spiritual appraises all things" (1 Cor. 2:15).

In dealing with the complex subject of Freemasonry, I feel we should examine the background of the organization. I remember well, as a young boy, cycling in my home county of Yorkshire, in England. I used to make trips over to the other side of Leeds, still in Yorkshire, to a place called Temple Newsom—perhaps the name or place is unfamiliar to you, but this is "Brönte" country.

Temple Newsom was on a hill, hidden in the woods, just the place for us boys to play Robin Hood and the

knights of the Crusades. I remember as if it was yester-
day, climbing in among the graves of the knights, trying
to decipher the names and seeing strange markings on
each and every tombstone. The knights, if you know
English and Middle Ages history, came to England and
Scotland, having been banished from the continent, Spain
in particular, and settled in Britain in the fourteenth century.

It was not until twenty years later, at my initiation as
an Entered Apprentice in a Masonic lodge, near
Downpatrick, in Northern Ireland, that I was taken aback
to see displayed on top of the open Bible, on the altar,
the symbols I had seen on those grave stones in England.
But, here they were displayed as instruments of Freemasonry. They were the legs of a man overlapping the woman
in the sexual position of the square and compass! I can
tell you; I was shattered!

It was not this revelation alone that jolted me because
I knew, within the first ten minutes into the First Degree,
that I had broken most of God's commandments! I made
no pretense in those days of being a Christian. However,
with my Church of England background, I knew enough
of the Bible to know that the blood oaths I was required
to swear, in fact any oaths, are against God's Holy Law.
Just making an oath, not knowing what it is about, is
against any national constitution, and we had the Magna
Carta!

Any Mason who calls himself a Christian and lies
about the compatibility of Freemasonry and Jesus Christ
is paving the road to hell unless he repents. I knew as a
non-Christian that what I was doing was evil. Those Masons who use the name of Christ to defend Freemasonry
are committing blasphemy.

From the background of the occult Knights Templars
came strong influence in the early formation of English
Freemasonry. That was blended with the Illuminati of
Adam Weishaupt from Germany and laced with the occult theology of Hinduism, brought over from India in
the sixteenth century by the British Raj.

Freemasonry, or the stone masons, was licensed at the guildhall. This is in the city of London, as were other guilds. For example, the Tanners' guild were workers in leather, the Weavers' guild were those who made cloth. All were "guilded," or made into guilds, and still remain licensed to this present day. The lord mayor of London is responsible to the queen from his palace at the guildhall. His home is the Mansion House in the city of London. These city guilds were the very first unions that we know of today.

The guilds held their meetings in the taverns or "pubs" of London. The very first record of a Masonic meeting was in a tavern in the city in 1717. In 1726, the lodges of London and the provinces combined to form the Grand Lodge of England. Freemasonry was thus formed officially. Other Grand Lodges were formed; my own constitution, where I became a Mason, was formed in Dublin in 1725, the following year, in Scotland, then Europe.

The French were always a bit strange to the British. They still are; not many people like the Channel Tunnel. We remember all the wars we have fought and won against the French. Today, the French Grand Lodge of the Orient is out of bounds to members of the English constitution.

I attended the Grand Lodge of England in Great Queen Street, near Trafalgar Square, for many years. There are about forty rooms—lodges—that hold meetings every day of the week except Sunday. There are as many banqueting rooms where you go to eat, drink, and talk business after lodge, but you never speak about Jesus Christ.

I travelled down to London in my dinner jacket, always in evening dress. I carried my little oblong attache case, which had in it my aprons, cuffs, and white cotton gloves, always worn in the lodge in Europe. My sashes, and my jewels, the latter for my giving to the Royal Masonic Hospital, Masonic girls' and Masonic boys' schools.

English Freemasonry is expensive. Twenty-five dollars for dinner after lodge meetings, and that was over twenty years ago! My dues to the lodges I belonged to kept me continually "in the red" with my bank. And, it stayed this way until I was set free years later!

There are no rings or tie pins in English Freemasonry, nothing to tell you are a Mason except as I say when you went to the Grand Lodge. There are no cars covered with Masonic emblems as we have in the United States. Freemasonry is supposed to be secret, didn't you know?

The extraordinary popularity of Freemasonry and its imitators here in America—whose love of secret societies exceeds that of any other country except China—can be attributed to the fact that Americans are extremely friendly, outgoing, and will join anything! I think it's partly out of a subconscious desire to escape the matriarchal influence, so much stronger here than in my homeland, and partly perhaps due to the absence of the glamour of pageantry of royalty and hereditary titles, and your less colorful and historic ceremony in connection with government, national and municipal occasions. The differences between what we call English Masonry and American Masonry also appears in the structure, the ritual and the ceremonies. Allow me to deal with the more important differences that I see, or rather saw.

The three craft degrees form the basis of the whole Masonic system as practiced in what used to be the countries of the British Empire. Together with Royal Arch, they form the sum total of Freemasonry as officially recognized by the English Grand Lodge. It is a fact that the majority of English Masons go no further than these degrees.

I found, as an English Mason, that there was a strong tendency to look down on the so-called higher degrees as a modern fancy innovation, which is no part of the pure and ancient Masonry. This, of course, is true, for the most part, for the other lodges I attended worldwide. I visited many countries and lived in some, and, in most lodges, there was a demonstration of the three tracing boards, unknown perhaps in the American Freemasonry. These presentations were by one selected person who has to completely memorize about three quarters of an hour of strict ritual applied to each of the three degrees.

The most popular degrees in the English constitution seem to be Mark Mason, Knights Templar, and Rose Croix, which is the eighteenth degree of what is called the Ancient and Accepted Rite. You have to have a Master Mason's certificate from either the English, Scottish, or Irish constitution for advancement into any other system. The degrees, all thirty of them, beginning with the fourth, that of Secret Master, and culminating in the Thirty-third Degree of Grand Inspector General, are controlled not by the United Grand Lodge of England, but by the Supreme Council at St. James in Piccadilly, London.

So, here you have a secret society within a secret society, a great difference compared with the structure here in America. It was on 5 December 1952 that His Royal Highness, the duke of Edinburgh, was initiated into my sister lodge, the Navy Lodge No. 2612. This was because of pressure from his future father-in-law, the then King George VI.

Her Majesty, Queen Elizabeth, now the duke's wife, is the Grand Patroness of Freemasonry, but is not allowed into a Masonic lodge. Her cousin, the duke of Kent, became the Grand Master of English Freemasonry at its 250th celebration. We have just witnessed the 275th anniversary celebration in the United Kingdom. The *Scottish Rite Journal* had a special feature on this.

Prince Charles has had great pressure put upon him to become a Freemason. He has refused point blank, saying, "I do not wish to join any secret society." The fact that he is deeply into New Age does not seem to worry him or the Royal Family. If the prince is initiated, to follow tradition, it is expected that he will join the lodge I attended, Royal Air Force Lodge No. 7335, in the Grand Lodge chambers in Great Queen Street. There is yet no indication Charles will change his attitude. The brother of the duke of Kent is also a Mason.

It does not take much intelligence to see why the Royal Family and Great Britain is in such a mess. The

curse of Freemasonry has been upon the family, especially since the first days of Masonry in Britain with the
then prince of Wales who became George III and was the
first Royal Grand Master of English Freemasonry.

The duke of Kent is only a Master Mason. The ambi-
tions, then, of the English Freemason is not rank, as it is
here in the states, but having the good fortune to become
an officer in his home lodge where he was initiated and
eventually to take the chair as Worshipful Master.

I never had the chance of "taking the chair," as it is
called, simply due to my nomadic Royal Air Force life
since I was unable to attend any lodge long enough to go
through the rungs of the ladder leading up to Worshipful
Master. The average time in England to become Worshipful Master is seven to ten years, and remember you have
to physically go through each degree in English Masonry.
There is no going up to Washington, D.C., to purchase
your degrees up to your Thirty-second Degree.

No wonder English Masons seemed to be old men!
The English system is indeed complex. Let me deal with
one major point here. The Shriners are purely American.
Millions of Americans have demonstrated their retarded
adolescence by being Nobles of the Mystic Shrine. Crippled
children may well rise up and call the Shriners "blessed"
even after a large percentage of the money the Shriners
take in goes towards the upkeep of their temples, bars,
golf courses, and those stupid toy cars. There are surely
other ways that are more becoming to band men together
in a spirit of benevolence. They could try Jesus Christ.

The blood oaths in the first three degrees and that of
the Master Elect have been taken out of the English constitution. They were removed after a United Grand Lodge
meeting held on 11 June 1986. I now understand that Jao
Bul On (the Masonic name for God in the Royal Arch)
was taken out of the Grand Lodge in February 1989.

I cannot emphasize too strongly that there are key
differences between United States and English Masonry.
There are different workings, as I have alluded to, within
the English constitution. Aldersgate (city of London), Ox-

ford, Bristol, and Metropolitan are just a few. There is, then, no absolute uniformity in Masonic workings. As long as the general structure is the same, and the landmarks of Masonry are preserved, verbal and ceremonial differences do not matter. Let's move from England; forgive me, but I felt you should have a fair knowledge of what used to be known as the "Mother of Freemasonry."

Years ago, as a zealous Freemason, I was given the original degree rituals of "Mother Killwining Lodge," the number two lodge of Scotland. They were given to me by a dear Scotsman whose ancestors had written them down in about 1720. I destroyed this document, which I now recognize as priceless, along with all my Masonic regalia and books when I came to Christ. I do remember that in this document, which was a word-for-word degree ritual, that there was no reference to Jesus Christ. I say this because this particular document was written at the very first meeting of Freemasonry.

I have said that places that were under the British Empire, by and large, work under the English constitution such as Malta, India, Malaysia, Hong Kong, and Singapore. A few of us in the ministry to Masons have been conducting correspondence with Christopher Hoffner, who has become the Worshipful Master of a lodge in Hong Kong. Hoffner has written many books, including some on Freemasonry. His latest, *Workman Unashamed*, is the testimony of a Christian Freemason, naturally received a great accolade in the *Scottish Rite Journal*. Hoffner has the single honor of being a full member of Quator Coronati Lodge of London—the world premier lodge of Masonic research. He also belongs to lodges of research in Hong Kong, Ireland, Maine, California, and New York. That's a very impressive record: I have never in all my life met or know of any Mason under such great bondage as Christopher Hoffner. Only the prayers of the saints will break him down.

Australia has now gone over to an Americanized Masonry, due no doubt to the influx of American soldiers in WWII and the R&R of American troops from Korea and Vietnam. They are trying to become a republic to sever the ties with Britain. The Australians, though, have now taken the blood oaths out of the Scottish and York Rites and in the three degrees and Master Elect, the same as in Britain.

This is a major step, yet it is not reported on in the *Scottish Rite Journal.* I wonder why! There is one lodge left in Sydney working under the Irish constitution. New Zealand is still working in the English constitution; that is as far as I can gather at this time. There is a great conflict building within Masonry, caused in a large part by the recent exposure of their innermost cultic secrets by zealots.

Possibly one of the highlights of my Masonic career was becoming a member of the prodigious Lodge Singapore. It was one of the wealthiest lodges in the Far East, and the world, perhaps, even after the Roman Catholic P2 Lodge in the Vatican. We always had five volumes of the Sacred Law displayed, five books of the five different religions that were always present in Lodge Singapore.

When I was a member, I recall that the Worshipful Master was a Moslem friend of mine, the police chief of Singapore. The Senior Warden was a Hindu, the Junior Warden a Chinese Taoist, the Inner Guard was a Buddhist, and lots of Past Masters were there who called themselves "Christians." The Quran for the Moslem to swear upon, the Veda for the Hindu's, the KeJi-Ki, the Records of Ancient Matters for the Shinto Japanese, the Tao-Teh-King, the classics of Taoism for the Chinese, books for the Jains, and Confucianism for the Buddhists are always available for the initiation ceremonies to be used at our meetings. But, no Jesus Christ!

The ritual of the First, Second, and Third Degrees have never instructed its members that Jesus Christ is the only mediator between God and men. It never tells them they can't truthfully call God their Father until they have a relationship with His Son; it does not tell them that it is impossible to build their spiritual house until they ask Jesus Christ to forgive them of their sins and He helps to build it; and they are never told that a man can never do enough good deeds or live a pure enough life to gain admission into the celestial lodge above.

In those first charges from the Scottish Mother Killwining Lodge, the number two lodge in the world, Jesus Christ was not recognized at the very start of Freemasonry, and He is not recognized as the Son of God, today.

In Germany, Freemasonry is mainly American. This was the first time I saw the "Top Hat" worn by the Worshipful Master. It has never been worn in Britain, but, of course, it is common here in America. Freemasonry in Italy became part of the Scottish Rite in the early days of Albert Pike and his friend from the occult, Giuseppe Mazzine. Most of Italy works in the Scottish Rite under the Grand Orient, which is *not* recognized by English Freemasonry.

To cover the continent of Africa would be a mammoth job here. Egyptian Masonry is steeped in the occult, more so than the Grand Orient. Moslem nations have Freemasonry, but no branches for women. If you have any understanding of Islam, you know why. I was a member of a Scottish lodge while living in Zambia, Central Africa. Again, nations that were under British rule tend to follow the constitutions of Great Britain. South Africa, in the main, works under the U.K. constitutions. Nearer home, Canada had the first lodge working under the Massachusetts Jurisdiction in 1749.

Incidentally, the oldest Masonic lodge room in the United States of America dates from 1760 at Prentise House, Massachusetts. Freemasonry crossed the Atlantic to the colonies of the old empire very early on, but the British, as founders of Freemasonry, remained the leading propagandist for the movement throughout the nineteenth and early twentieth centuries.

Albert Pike put a stop to this in the acceptance of Scottish Rite through *Morals and Dogmas*, what American Masonry loves to call "The Mother of All Freemasonry!" There are possibly more lodges in the world now working under the Scottish Jurisdiction than any other constitution or jurisdiction. I have tried to give you the basic background of international Freemasonry and how it has developed through most of the countries of the world.

I leave you with this. Even after I had returned to the faith of my youth and had come out from among the darkness of Eastern Mysticism and left behind the Quran and its teachings of Mohammed and the Bhagavad of Hinduism, I was still in a spiritual battle for my life. My standard was now the Holy Bible and Jesus Christ. I knew that there was no other way to God, but there was no fullness to my walk. I read one day where Jesus said: "You call me Jesus, your savior, your Lord—yet you practice things I have not taught you. Depart from me, I never knew you, you workers of evil" (Matt. 7: 21-3).

I had not found that yearned for one-on-one walk with Jesus even though I had asked for advice from almost everyone I knew. I had no answers. I finally got down on my knees and asked Jesus what was wrong. One word came back to me, as though shouted from heaven, "Masonry!" I knew I was still in trouble with the real God. As if I needed confirmation, a letter came from our daughter in London. In it, she said, "You have to get out of Masonry, Daddy! You know it is evil, and you'll never walk with God until you do." That was the day I burned all my Masonic regalia. Everything was burnt to ashes before me.

After all my wanderings and searching, I was finally able to separate myself from the spirits of darkness, to ask God's forgiveness, and repent before Him of the evil in which I had been a participant. And, He heard my cry, for I felt the weight of all that evil lift off me, and, for the first time in my life, I knew I was free. When you are set free in Jesus, you are set free, indeed (John 8:36).

Six

The Secret Doctrine

Larry Kunk

Does the Masonic lodge have a secret doctrine that is known by only those at the top of the organization? If knowledge of a secret doctrine were not restricted to only those in the higher degrees, how would the lodge select which men were to have access to those secret teachings? What methods would be used to promote, while at the same time restrict, such sensitive information?

If there were a secret doctrine, would it be possible to accurately know its teachings without joining the organization? Most Masons, even those in the higher degrees, will be quick to deny the existence of any secret doctrine.

Many Masons have claimed that the ritual is all that there is. Is that really true? Are Masonic teachings limited to ritual, or are there teachings beyond the ritual that Masonry attempts to convey to its members? To answer those questions, we must turn to the writings of Masonic authorities.

The Highest Authority of Freemasonry

Many times, Masons have claimed that the ritual is the only authority of Freemasonry. In examining that claim, we need to acknowledge that the rituals of the

125

degrees of Freemasonry were written by men. Is it reasonable to assign higher authority to a work than is given its author or authors? Obviously those who wrote the rituals have, or had, a greater level of authority than the rituals that they produced. If we could identify the authors of the rituals, we would unquestionably identify men who are Masonic authorities. It would be very difficult today to identify all of the authors of the rituals of the three degrees of the Blue Lodge. The ritual was not written all at once, but evolved over time.[1]

The major portions of the ritual are well over one hundred years old. All of the major authors are dead. However, it is quite easy to identify those who have the ability to alter the ritual as practiced in lodges today. Any Grand Lodge has the authority to alter the ritual that is practiced in its jurisdiction. There are portions of ritual, called landmarks, which Grand Lodges will never alter in any significant way. But, there is some divergence of opinion among various Grand Lodges as to which actually do constitute all of the true landmarks of Freemasonry. According to the *Indiana Monitor and Freemason's Guide*, there are seven that are universally accepted.[2]

An example of one of those seven landmarks is the Legend of the Third Degree. The Legend of the Third Degree cannot be significantly altered without altering the nature of Freemasonry. However, less essential portions of the ritual can be, and have been, altered by ruling Grand Lodges. An example that demonstrates that the ritual can be changed has been provided by the Grand Lodge of England. In recent times, the Grand Lodge of England removed the blood oaths from the ritual of the Blue Lodge. Obviously, since a Grand Lodge has the ability to alter ritual, it has higher authority than the ritual. The ritual is the product of an authority or authorities.

Another means of determining with whom the highest authority rests is to consider the process by which a new lodge is formed. In the United States, the practice is for the Grand Master to issue a dispensation to operate until the ensuing Grand Lodge at which the dispensation may be continued, a charter may be granted, or the dispensation dismissed.[3]

Since the Grand Lodges are the highest authorities of Masonry, Grand Lodge publications produced for use by Masons, including Masonic monitors, books of Masonic law, and training materials, are excellent sources of authoritative Masonic teaching. Other written materials that are listed as recommended reading in Grand Lodge publications, which are produced for consumption by Masons, would also be excellent sources of Masonic information.

There are forty-nine Grand Lodges in the United States, one in each of the forty-eight continental states and one in the District of Columbia.[4] Alaska and Hawaii fall under the jurisdictions of the Grand Lodges of Washington and California, respectively. Many Masonic bodies have official periodical publications, which provide a window into the Masonic system.

The Training Process of Grand Lodges

Lodge training methods, in general, are variations on a theme. The general method is to conduct the candidate through the ritual and explain to him that the ritual has meanings that he can only know if he discovers them through his own efforts. The lodge never tells a candidate directly what the complete meaning of the ritual is.

A series of booklets have been compiled by the Committee on Masonic Education of the Grand Lodge of Iowa for use in educating the new Mason. The booklets are titled *On the Threshold*, *The Entered Apprentice*, *The Fellow Craft*, and *The Master Mason*. They have been adopted and republished by Grand Lodges in other states, including Indiana and North Carolina. The Indiana version has been through multiple printings. These training materials can be given to new members as they progress through the first three degrees of the Blue Lodge. The first booklet, *On the Threshold*, is given to the newly elected member before he receives the Entered Apprentice De-

gree. After each degree is conferred, the booklet with the
same name is then presented to the man. These particular booklets are not used in all jurisdictions. Their con-
tent is congruent with other Masonic writings. As we shall
see, some Grand Lodges use other tools to achieve the
same end.

Most Grand Lodges produce a monitor, which is given
to each new member. The names of the monitors vary
from state to state. In Virginia, it is called the *Virginia
Text Book*. In West Virginia, the monitor is titled *Masonic
Text Book*. In Georgia, the monitor is titled *Masonic Manual
and Code*. The Grand Lodge of Indiana publishes the
Indiana Monitor and Freemason's Guide, which must be
given to each man when he is raised to Master Mason.
That requirement is Masonic law in the state of Indiana.[5]

The term *raised* is used in the same sense as raised
from the dead. In the *Indiana Monitor and Freemason's
Guide*, under "Declaration of Principles," the Grand Lodge
states, "It is a social organization only so far as it fur-
nishes additional inducement that men may forgather in
numbers, thereby providing more material for its primary
work of education, of worship, and of charity."[6] The monitor published by the Grand Lodge of Indiana tells new
Master Masons that the lodge is not primarily a social
organization; its primary purpose is education, worship,
and charity. Many Masons have claimed that the lodge is
simply a social organization. And, in a footnote at the
bottom of the page, the Grand Lodge explains the purpose of the Declaration of Principles: "In order to correct
any misunderstanding and to refute willful misrepresen-
tation, this Declaration of Principles was adopted by the
Grand Lodge of Indiana on May 24, 1939."[7]

The Grand Lodge of Indiana wants each Mason to
know that its primary purpose is education, worship, and
charity. Furthermore, the lodge makes it clear that any
social nature is strictly for the purpose of enlarging membership. The *Masonic Manual and Code*, published by the
Grand Lodge of Georgia, contains the same Declaration
of Principles.[8]

The declaration was formulated in February, 1939, by the Grand Masters Conference in Washington, D.C.[9] The Declaration of Principles was widely accepted and is used by many Grand Lodges.

Masonic monitors often contain footnotes or text that uplift prominent Masonic authors or books. The favorable mention of a Masonic author in a monitor would lead many to believe that the Grand Lodge was endorsing the writings of those authors. An example is the following text from the *Masonic Text Book*[10] for use in the lodges of West Virginia: "Brother Albert Pike, one of the most illustrious Masons in all the ages, and who was an acknowledged authority upon all Masonic questions, was a believer in ancient Landmarks."[11]

The *Indiana Monitor and Freemason's Guide* mentions Masonic historian H.L. Haywood and James E. Craig as prominent modern authors.[12] Haywood gives a very truthful description of the purpose of the lodge in his book *The Great Teachings of Masonry*. In it, Haywood wrote, "The Fraternity itself exists in order to keep fixed on a man a certain set of influences, and in order to bring about certain changes in the world, etc.: its secrecy is a means to that end, and helps to make such a purpose possible."[13]

After the deeper meanings of the ritual are fully understood, the words of Haywood will take on an ominous meaning. Many statements in Masonic books cannot be properly understood by those not acquainted with the deeper meanings of the ritual. Masonic books contain teachings which go over the heads of most who read them, but to those who are familiar with the deeper meanings, the writings are easily understood.

Masonry's Most Important Symbol

Masonry is full of symbols. The most important of those symbols is discussed in a cursory way in the *Indiana Monitor and Freemason's Guide*: "The Legend of the Third Degree . . . is the most important and significant of the legendary symbols of Freemasonry. It has descended from age to age by oral tradition, and has been preserved in every Masonic rite, practiced in any country or language, with no essential alteration."[14]

The Legend of the Third Degree and the Significance of the Lost Word

The lost word, and the rediscovery of it, is a central theme in Masonic ritual. The setting for the legend is the building of Solomon's Temple, just before completion. In the ritual of the third degree, each man who is raised to Master Mason is required to portray Hiram Abiff, the Grand Master. For working on the temple, the Fellowcrafts are to receive the secrets of a Master Mason which will entitle them to the wages of a master. Some of the men do not want to wait until the appropriate time to obtain the secrets. Hiram Abiff is accosted by three men who are referred to in the ritual as the three ruffians. They are Jubela, Jubelo, and Jebulum. They demand that he reveal to them the secrets of a Master Mason.

Hiram Abiff is a righteous individual; he will not reveal the secrets to them until the proper time and place and then only in the presence of Hiram, king of Tyre, and Solomon, king of Israel. The first ruffian encounters Hiram Abiff at the south gate but fails to obtain the Master's word. The second ruffian encounters Hiram Abiff in the west and demands, "Give me the Master's word, or I will take your life in a moment!" The third ruffian engages Hiram Abiff in the east and does take his life. Hiram is unjustly murdered. When he died, the word was lost because it could not be mentioned except in the presence of the two Hirams and Solomon.

Hiram Abiff is buried on the brow of a hill west of Mount Moriah to conceal the crime and the three murderers attempt to flee the country. After King Solomon notices that Hiram Abiff is missing, a search is mounted. One of the searchers finds a fresh grave. The body is confirmed to be that of Grand Master Hiram Abiff.

At the grave site, King Solomon (the Worshipful Master) declares that the Master's word has been lost. He declares that the first word spoken after the body is raised will be adopted for the regulation of the Masters' lodges until future generations shall find the right word. King Solomon instructs the Entered Apprentices and the Fellowcrafts to attempt to raise the body of Hiram.

They fail to resurrect their master from the dead. They are unable to raise Hiram because the "flesh cleaves from the bone." The Worshipful Master makes the attempt, and Hiram Abiff is then raised from the dead by the strong grip of the lions paw of the tribe of Judah. (Jesus is the *real* lion of the tribe of Judah.)

The first word spoken after Hiram is raised from the dead is spoken on the five points of fellowship. The word is Mah-Hah-Bone; it is the substitute for the lost word to be used until the lost word is again found.

The Meaning of the Legend of the Third Degree

What is the meaning of the ritual? The *Indiana Monitor and Freemason's Guide* has the following to say about the meaning of the Legend of the Third Degree:

> It was the single object of all the ancient rites and mysteries practiced in the very bosom of pagan darkness, shining as a solitary beacon in all that surrounding gloom, and cheering the philosopher in his weary pilgrimage of life, to teach the immortality of the soul. This is still the great design of the third degree of Masonry. This is the scope and aim of its ritual. The Master Mason represents man, when youth, manhood, old age, and life itself have passed away as fleeting shadows, yet raised from the grave of iniquity, and quickened into another and better existence. By its legend and all its ritual, it is implied that we have been redeemed from the death of sin and the sepulchre of pollution. (144–5)

The paragraph from the Indiana monitor was written by Albert G. Mackey, one of Masonry's most respected authors. The text is found in Mackey's book, *Manual of the Lodge*.[15] By mandating that each man be given a copy of the monitor, the Grand Lodge of Indiana is really telling every new Master Mason raised in Indiana that the ritual implies that they have been redeemed from the death of sin.

Anything that is said to redeem a man from the death of sin can only properly be described as a plan of salvation. The Grand Lodge of Indiana does not use the word *salvation*, yet it is obviously implied and is found in the original source, *Manual of the Lodge*: "The Master Mason represents a man saved from the grave of iniquity, and raised to the faith of salvation."[16]

Although *Manual of the Lodge* was written over 130 years ago, it is still in print! It is reproduced completely in the *Ahiman Rezon*, the Masonic monitor published by the authority of the Grand Lodge of South Carolina. The statement that the Master Mason represents a man saved from the grave of iniquity and raised to the faith of salvation is also found in the *North Carolina Lodge Manual*, published by the Grand Lodge of North Carolina.

The *Monitor and Ceremonies, Ancient, Free, and Accepted Masons*, published by the order of the Grand Lodge of Nebraska, also contains Mackey's teachings concerning salvation. Mackey's writings from *Manual of the Lodge* are reproduced faithfully. Obviously Albert Mackey is a Masonic authority whose writings concerning salvation have been endorsed by Grand Lodges.

Masonic monitors provide evidence that many Grand Lodges, the highest authorities of Freemasonry, currently teach that the Master Mason has been redeemed from the death of sin. The Master Mason is said to represent a man saved from the grave of iniquity and raised to the faith of salvation. There are other writings found in Masonic monitors that would encourage a Mason to believe that he has salvation or that he will go to heaven when his days on earth come to an end. Consider the following two passages:

> The covering of a Lodge is a clouded canopy, or
> star-decked heaven, where all good Masons hope
> at last to arrive. . . .

We should apply our knowledge to the discharge of our respective duties, to God, our neighbors and ourselves, so that in age, as Master Masons, we may enjoy the happy reflections consequent on a well-spent life, and die in the hope of a glorious immortality.

The two passages above are found without significant variation in the monitors of Alabama, Florida, Georgia, Idaho, Illinois, Indiana, Kansas, Kentucky, Michigan, Minnesota, Mississippi, Nebraska, North Carolina, Ohio, Tennessee, South Carolina, Texas, Virginia and West Virginia.[17]

The monitor from Texas contains only a portion of the latter passage. Monitors from nineteen states were checked. Since all that were checked contained the two passages, it is statistically reasonable to assume that the vast majority, if not all, of the monitors of other states will also contain them.

What is the common source of the text? The first passage is from the ritual of Entered Apprentice Degree, while the second passage is from the ritual of the Master Mason Degree. During the Third Degree ritual, just before Hiram Abiff is raised from the dead, the Worshipful Master offers a prayer which ends with the following: "Yet, O Lord! have compassion on the children of thy creation, administer them comfort in time of trouble, and save them with an everlasting salvation. Amen. So mote it be." No Mason can truthfully say that the lodge does not hold out the hope of salvation to the Master Mason. The man who has not been in the lodge in years, and probably doesn't remember ritual clearly, can check his monitor and verify that Masonry teaches that the Master Mason may expect salvation.

Master Masons include Moslems, Hindus, Buddhists, Mormons, members of Christian churches, and some who have no religious affiliation other than the lodge. Masonry requires only a belief in a deity. Moslems, Hindus, Buddhists, and Mormons all reject the unique Deity of Jesus Christ. Since Masonry teaches that Master Masons, as a class, are redeemed from the death of sin, raised to the faith of salvation, many die in the vacant hope of a glorious immortality.

Masonry is claiming one of the following to be true:

1. Something is brought about in the making of a Master Mason which provides salvation.

2. All men who believe in a deity have salvation, regardless of the identity of that deity.

Either teaching is unacceptable to a Christian. The Mason who professes to be Christian is presented with a bit of a dilemma. Can a man be a Christian and at the same time embrace an organization which gives assurance of salvation on terms other than faith in Jesus Christ? What will Jesus say?

The Education Process Continued

The ritual of Freemasonry, as well as the writings in the monitors, assures the Master Mason of salvation. However, the ritual and the monitors do not explain exactly how the Master Mason is to be saved. The deeper meanings of the rituals contained in the secret teachings are concealed from some, while revealed to others. What does the Grand Lodge of Indiana do to encourage the new Master Mason to discover the deeper meanings behind the ritual? In the *Indiana Monitor and Freemason's Guide*, the Grand Lodge of Indiana states, "In the ceremonies of making a Mason, we do not attempt to do more than to indicate the pathway to Masonic knowledge, to lay the foundation for the Masonic edifice. The brother must pursue the journey or complete the structure for himself by reading and reflection."[18]

Clearly, the Grand Lodge of Indiana advises all Master Masons that they are not being given all of the significant knowledge about Freemasonry. They are told that they must read and reflect upon what they have read to obtain complete understanding. Which books should a Mason read to learn about Freemasonry? Obviously, those written by Masonic authors. But, some Masons don't spend the time to do the required reading to complete the structure or to develop an in-depth knowledge of Freemasonry. In their ignorance, they are unaware of how much they don't know. Those who do spend the time to do the research necessary to understand the deeper things of the craft are bound by oath not to reveal them to non-Masons. Each man determines for himself if he will gain access to additional Masonic teachings or not. If he is excluded from additional knowledge, it is because he has not made the effort to read and reflect.

Various Methods Used by Other Grand Lodges

The monitors used in Ohio lodges are not as detailed as those of Indiana, South Carolina, and some other states. *Masonic Lodge Methods* by L. B. Blakemore, a Past Grand Master of Ohio, discusses the importance of the lodge library and suggests the following:

> It is suggested that when a Candidate has been Raised, and while he is still in the Master's care, the Lodge Librarian, or the Chaplain, or the Master himself should address him somewhat as follows: "I herewith present you with a Masonic book which I have borrowed for you from our Lodge Library (or other Masonic Library). You will read it and return it and secure another one and so continue your search for more light in Masonry." This is impressive and figures in the Candidate's mind as a part of his Initiation and starts him out on a search for more "Masonic Light" and information. The book presented should be an interesting one—carefully selected with a view to his ability to appreciate it. (L. B. Blakemore, *Masonic Lodge Methods* [Richmond, VA: Macoy Publishing & Masonic Supply Co., 1953], 43–4)

The practice of giving a book to a new Master Mason rather than lending one from the lodge library is also common. Macoy Publishing and Masonic Supply Company's September 1992 catalog names *The Builders*[19] as one of the outstanding classics in Masonic literature. The catalog goes on to say that many Grand Lodges

present a copy to each newly raised Mason. Evidence of
that fact was found in a copy of *The Builders*. The book-
plate states, "Presented to [the man's name] on being
raised to the Sublime Degree of Master Mason." It was
signed by the Master of a Wisconsin lodge.

The *Builders* and its author, Joseph Fort Newton, are
listed in footnotes and text in Masonic monitors from
various states. In the *Indiana Monitor and Freemason's Guide*,
a long quote from *The Builders* is reproduced. The text
just prior to the quote identifies the author and title of
the book and states that "it bids fair to become a Masonic
classic."[20]

The *Kentucky Monitor* also contains a long quote from
The Builders. The quote is used to answer the question,
When is a man a Mason? Just before the quote, which is
used to answer the question, the *Kentucky Monitor* states,
"There is no satisfactory formula. . . . Dr. Joseph Fort
Newton, in his Masonic classic, 'The Builders' at least
expresses its true philosophy when he says: . . ."[21]

When Grand Lodges take writings of a particular man
for use in Masonic monitors, they themselves do not author
that portion of the monitor but grant authority to those
who wrote the quoted text. In the act of quoting, the
Grand Lodge acknowledges the author to be an accepted
source of accurate Masonic information. In other words,
the Grand Lodge identifies the author being quoted as a
Masonic authority. Denials that Masonic authors who are
quoted in official Grand Lodge publications are authorities on Freemasonry ring hollow.

The Masonic training booklets, which were compiled
by the Committee on Masonic Education, and have been
reprinted by various Grand Lodges, stress the importance of the writings of Masonic authors. The final booklet, *The Master Mason*, contains the following:

> It is safe to say that among the countless thou-
> sands who have in the past been raised to the
> Sublime Degree of Master Mason, no one of them
> realized at the time the full implications of the
> ceremony. This clearly would be impossible. Yet it

is vitally important that the deeper meanings of this degree be understood if one is to become a Master Mason in fact as well as in name. (Authorized by Grand Lodge F. & A.M. of Indiana, The Master Mason [Franklin, Indiana: The Indiana Masonic Home], 2)

The Master Mason has been authorized and is used by multiple Grand Lodges, including those of Iowa, Indiana, and North Carolina. The Grand Lodges teach that a man cannot become a Master Mason in fact, as well as in name, until he knows the deeper meanings of the Master Mason Degree. The implications of such a teaching are significant. If Master Masons, as a class, have salvation, then, unless a particular man was a Master Mason in fact as well as in name, he would not necessarily have salvation. The instruction continues:

This final booklet is intended to indicate something of what lies beyond the instruction you have already received. If it encourages you to investigate still further it will indeed have served a good purpose. The literature of Masonry in all its many phases is within your reach and your Worshipful Master or Secretary can give you particulars. (2)

Your enjoyment of Freemasonry, its value to you in your future life, your contribution to the fulfillment of its great mission, will be in direct proportion to your understanding of its secrets, which, if you recall the degree through which you have just passed, you do not yet have and which can only be gained by your own endeavors and the assistance of your brethren. . . . Much has been written of Freemasonry. Probably your own Lodge possesses a library of books telling of the history of Freemasonry and treating of its philosophy, symbolism, and jurisprudence. These books are at your disposal at all times and there are many others that you may purchase for study in your own home. (3–4)

Clearly, the Grand Lodges using these booklets are endorsing use of the lodge library as a means to becoming a Master Mason in fact, as well as one in name. The Grand Lodges also state that many of the Masonic books, which they would have a new Master Mason read to gain an understanding of the deeper meanings, are available for purchase.

A Non-Mason Can Understand the Secrets of Masonry

The rituals of the first three degrees have been thoroughly revealed and are available in written form to anyone who has an interest in them. Masonic books which are found in lodge libraries are available from a number of sources. An individual who is not a Mason can read and reflect and come to a very detailed understanding of Masonic teachings. The primary criteria should be to identify those materials that are produced for the consumption of Masons by a credible Masonic authority and that are distributed throughout the Masonic system with the knowledge and cooperation of ruling Masonic bodies such as a Grand Lodge.

Discovering the Deeper Meaning

If the new Mason raised in Indiana diligently read all of the materials issued to him by the Grand Lodge of Indiana, it would be reasonable for him to start his search for the deeper meanings of the ritual by obtaining a copy of *The Builders* by Joseph Fort Newton. It is endorsed as a classic in both the Indiana and Kentucky monitors. Many Grand Lodges present a copy of it to the new Master Mason. *The Builders* is the first Masonic book not published by a Grand Lodge that many Masons read. *The Builders* contains a chapter which is titled "The Secret Doctrine." The chapter title gives away the fact that the Masonic lodge does indeed have a secret doctrine. Current editions contain a seven-page bibliography that points the seeking Mason to Masonic books that explain the secret doctrine in detail. Several of the Masonic books used here to document the secret doctrine are listed in the bibliography in *The Builders*.

Tying the Existence of a Secret Doctrine to the Grand Lodge

Indirectly tying the existence of the secret doctrine back to the Grand Lodge of Indiana and many other states is not difficult. When a Masonic monitor or other Grand Lodge publication uses quotes from *The Builders* or declares that it is a Masonic classic, an indirect link between the secret doctrine and the Grand Lodge has been created. Finding a direct link between the secret doctrine and a Grand Lodge is more difficult.

It would appear that a direct link exists in the *Kentucky Monitor*. The thirteenth edition of the *Kentucky Monitor* contains an index that lists secret doctrine among the entries. Seventeen pages are listed as having information about the secret doctrine. The most direct passage is found in a preface entitled "The Spirit of Masonry": "This, in short, is a synopsis of the story that Masonry attempts to tell, the Secret Doctrine, completed from the wisdom of the ancient East."[22]

Most of the text referring to the secret doctrine on those seventeen pages of the *Kentucky Monitor* is similar to the following two passages:

> Masonry has been defined as a beautiful system of morality, veiled in allegory and illustrated by symbols. Now an allegory is a story told to illustrate or convey some truth. Some of the most important truths have been handed down to us through allegories, that being one of the favorite methods of the Master used to convey His teachings. It is one of the peculiarities of an allegory that its message may not be understood by all men. One must be prepared within his own mind and heart to receive the truth or else he sees it not. It is only a few of all those who hear who perceive the lesson designed to be taught by the allegory. The great majority, having ears to hear, hear not; having

eyes to see, see not the beautiful lesson but hear
only a pretty story that interests for a short while
and then is lost. But the earnest seeker for truth,
he who is duly and truly prepared for its perception, sees beyond the veil of the allegory and per-
ceives the beautiful, simple truth which it conceals
from the multitude but reveals to the chosen
few. . . .

So, my brother, Masonry teaches by allegories and
symbols, and it is your part to extract from them
the truths that will be of service to you in the
building of an upright Masonic character. If you
perceive only the stories that Masonry presents to
you and do not see deeper into what they are
designed to teach, you will miss the most wonderful part of Masonry. (20–1)

Does this link the Grand Lodge of Kentucky directly
to the existence of a secret doctrine? Some would say no
because the *Kentucky Monitor* is not published directly by
the Grand Lodge of Kentucky. Yet, the *Kentucky Monitor*,
which was arranged by Henry Pirtle, has been presented
to new Master Masons in lodges throughout Kentucky for
more than fifty years. Pirtle is a Past Master, or former
Worshipful Master of the lodge. Like the *Indiana Monitor
and Freemason's Guide*, the *Kentucky Monitor* borrows much
of its verbiage from books written by Masonic authorities,
and those books and authors are often listed in footnotes.
Because the *Kentucky Monitor* is not published by the
Grand Lodge, it can be slightly more direct without link-
ing the Grand Lodge to the secret doctrine.

Others would say that it does directly link the Grand
Lodge of Kentucky to the existence of a secret doctrine
because the *Kentucky Monitor* is presented to every Master
Mason raised in the Bluegrass State. The Grand Lodge
obviously is aware of the contents of the monitor; it has
been in use for more than fifty years.

Many Grand Lodges direct that a copy of *The Builders*
be given to every new Master Mason. Some would say

that when a new Master Mason is given a copy of *The Builders* as part of his Third Degree ceremony a direct link to the existence of the secret doctrine is legally and legitimately formed. Obviously, if the teachings in *The Builders*, including the teaching of the existence of the secret doctrine, were not compatible with Freemasonry, Grand Lodges would not promote or distribute the book.

Understanding the Secret Doctrine Is Crucial to Understanding Freemasonry

Swinburne Clymer wrote in *The Mysticism of Masonry*, "The Secret Doctrine is the complete philosophy of Masonic Symbolism."[23] This statement is correct. The true nature of the Masonic lodge cannot be understood without understanding the secret doctrine and comparing it to the gospel of Jesus. Masonic author George Steinmetz wrote *The Lost Word: Its Hidden Meaning*. The jacket flap of the book contains a statement that the book was "Written with the primary purpose of delving into the Secret Doctrine in Freemasonry."[24]

In chapter two, titled "The Secret Doctrine," Steinmetz writes,

> The Secret Doctrine, being the real secret of Freemasonry, is not divulged even to the candidate. There is no machinery set up in the ritual for the purpose, and the Secret Doctrine itself is not even acknowledged to exist. . . . Officially, the ritual is "all that there is," and no Grand Lodge will go beyond that fact and attempt to define the teachings of Masonry, nor will any Grand Lodge (to my knowledge) admit the existence of the Secret Doctrine which is so openly discussed and written about by Masonic students and authorities on Masonic symbolism. (10-1)

Steinmetz continues:

> The Secret Doctrine in Freemasonry cannot be too strongly stressed. Firstly, because there are those, in the Order, who in their lack of knowl-

edge claim that it does not exist; secondly, because the seeking Mason can gain no further light than is shed by the ritual itself, until he starts his quest for the REAL SECRETS of the hidden Mysteries of Freemasonry—and they are found WITHIN THE SECRET DOCTRINE! (12-3)

After considering the writings of Steinmetz, the *Indiana Monitor and Freemason's Guide*, the *Kentucky Monitor*, and *Masonic Lodge Methods* by Blakemore, we gain a better understanding of the method. The lodge avoids directly referring to the secret doctrine. Instead, it tells the new Master Mason that there is more to learn and the way to learn is to read. This method of instruction provides Grand Lodges an ability to deny responsibility for the secret doctrine or even to deny the existence of the secret doctrine. Even as they deny the existence of the secret doctrine, they continue to encourage the discovery of it. Masonic practice casts serious doubt on the credibility of denials of either the existence of the secret doctrine, or that it accurately reflects Masonic teaching.

Additional Details of the
Meaning of the Legend of the Third Degree

The *Indiana Monitor and Freemason's Guide* stated of the Legend of the Third Degree: "By its legend and all its ritual, it is implied that we have been redeemed from the death of sin and the sepulchre of pollution."[25]

The *Indiana Monitor* makes the claim that Masons are redeemed from the death of sin, yet the monitor fails to explain the details of the salvation process. *Mystic Masonry* by J. D. Buck contains a more complete explanation of the meaning of the Legend of the Third Degree:

In the third degree the candidate impersonates Hiram, who has been shown to be identical with the Christos of the Greeks, and with the Sun-Gods of all other nations. The superiority of Masonry at this point over all exoteric Religions consists in this: All these religions take the symbol for the thing symbolized. Christ was originally like the father. Now He is made identical with the Father. In deifying Jesus the whole of humanity is bereft of Christos as an eternal potency within every human soul, a latent Christ in every man. In thus deifying one man, they have orphaned the whole of humanity! On the other hand, Masonry, in making every candidate personify Hiram, has preserved the original teaching, which is a universal glyphic. Few candidates may be aware that Hiram whom they have represented and personified is ideally, and precisely the same as Christ. Yet such is undoubtedly the case. This old philosophy shows what Christ as a glyphic means, and how the Christ-state results from real Initiation, or from the evolution of the human into the Divine. (J. D. Buck, *Mystic Masonry* [Chicago, IL: Charles T. Powner Company], 133-4)

The thrust of the paragraph is that Jesus is not unique. And, Buck further writes that Hiram Abiff is identical to Jesus Christ! Buck states that by declaring Jesus to be uniquely God, orthodox Christianity has deprived the whole of humanity from the possibility of becoming Christs! The Christ-state is said to be the goal for each man. Each Mason can evolve from the human into the divine through Masonic initiation! In other words, man can become God!

Most Masons will deny that this could be a viable explanation of the Legend of the Third Degree. Some are sincere and simply ignorant of the facts. A Master Mason who was raised in Kentucky claimed that he had never seen anything in his Masonic experience which would in any way agree with the interpretation of J. D. Buck. He claimed that none of the materials he had been given contained anything similar. The man said that he had not read any Masonic book other than the *Kentucky Monitor*, yet the *Kentucky Monitor* contains the following text in the preface. The context is a discussion of the religions of antiquity and how each believed in a mediator or redeemer.

All believed in a future life, to be attained by pu-
rification and trials; in a state or successive states
of reward and punishment; and in a Mediator or
Redeemer, by whom the Evil Principle was to be
overcome and the Supreme Deity reconciled to
His creatures. The belief was general that He was
to be born of a virgin and suffer a painful death.
The Hindus called him Krishna; the Chinese,
Kioun-tse; the Persians, Sosiosch; the Chaldeans,
Dhouvanai; the Egyptians, Horus; Plato, Love; the
Scandinavians, Balder; the Christians, Jesus; Ma-
sons, Hiram. It is interesting that the "small hill
west of Mount Moriah" has been identified as
Golgotha, or Mount Calvary. (XIV-XV)

The meaning of this paragraph in the *Kentucky Monitor* is clear. Jesus is the redeemer of Christians, and Hiram
is a redeemer for Masons! The *Kentucky Monitor* clearly
presents Hiram Abiff as being in the same classification
as Jesus! It even identifies the "small hill west of Mount
Moriah" with Calvary!

The *Ahiman Rezon*, the monitor of South Carolina,
supports the identification of Hiram with Jesus:

The small hill near Mount Moriah can be clearly
identified by the most convincing analogies as being
no other than Mount Calvary. . . . The Christian
Mason will readily perceive the peculiar character
of the symbolism which this identification of the
spot on which the great truth of the resurrection
was unfolded in both systems (the Masonic and
the Christian) must suggest. (147–8)

The preface to the *Kentucky Monitor* contains other
comparisons. In a discussion of the book of John, which
they say was written to prove the author's view of a con-
tested question, the following is found: "He commences
his essay, 'In the beginning was the Word, and the Word
was with God, and the Word was God.' Of course the
Word was lost at the death of the Christian's Redeemer,
Jesus, as at the death of Hiram."[26]

Jesus is the Word. The *Kentucky Monitor* states that the Word was lost when Jesus died. Christians know that Jesus is alive, and the Word was not lost. Jesus rose from the dead and stands victorious. They are clearly implying that Jesus is dead. The final portion from the preface of the *Kentucky Monitor*, which verifies the correctness of J. D. Buck's interpretation of the ritual, concerns the teaching that man can become God. From the *Kentucky Monitor*:

> The three really great rituals of the human race are the Präjápati ritual of ancient Hinduism, the Mass of the Christian Church, and the Third Degree of Masonry. Widely as they may differ in detail, and far apart as they may seem to be in externals, yet together they testify to the profoundest insight of the human soul: that God becomes man that man may become God! (XX)

There are at least two major issues to be considered here. First, the *Kentucky Monitor* agrees with Buck's interpretation that man can become God! The second is the implication that God (Jesus) became man and then became God. Jesus became man but, He never *became* God. He was *always* God. The implication that He became God is very close to implying that He became a Christ! It is equivalent to saying that Jesus was not Christ when He came in the flesh. The original source of this text is page 183 of *The Builders* by Joseph Fort Newton. Those lodges that present that book to new Master Masons are providing training materials that directly state that man can become God.

Additional details of the secret doctrine reveal the Masonic plan of salvation more completely. *Mystic Masonry* by J. D. Buck, M.D. contains a chapter titled "The Secret Doctrine." Buck writes:

Every soul must "work out its own salvation," and "take the Kingdom of Heaven by force." Salvation by faith and the vicarious atonement were not taught, as now interpreted, by Jesus, nor are these doctrines taught in the esoteric Scriptures. They are later and ignorant perversions of the original doctrines. In the Early Church, as in the secret doctrine, there was not one Christ for the whole world, but a potential Christ in every man. (57)

Later in the chapter, Buck further explains:

> It is far more important that men should strive to become Christs than that they should believe that Jesus was Christ. If the Christ-state can be attained by but one human being during the whole evolution of the race, then the evolution of man is a farce and human perfection an impossibility. Jesus is no less Divine because all men may reach the same Divine perfection. (62)

According to the secret doctrine, faith in Jesus the Christ is not necessary for salvation. Notice that in the secret doctrine, the meaning of Christ has been redefined. Instead of referring to the Messiah when they use the term, they refer to a state or condition which man can attain. The secret doctrine teaches that Jesus was Christ, but he was not the only one to attain that state. Being Christ is vital to Masonic salvation.

The secret doctrine states that each man must work out his own salvation. According to the secret doctrine, Jesus is not unique. He is just another man; all men can become Christs. But, the Bible says, "Jesus saith unto him, I am the way, the truth, and the life: no man cometh unto the Father, but by me" (John 14:6).

> Be it known unto you all, and to all the people of Israel, that by the name of Jesus Christ of Nazareth, whom ye crucified, whom God raised from the dead, even by him doth this man stand here before you whole. This is the stone which was set at nought of you builders, which is become the head of the corner. Neither is there salvation in any other: for there is none other name under heaven given among men, whereby we must be saved. (Acts 4:10-2)

> For all have sinned, and come short of the glory
> of God; Being justified freely by his grace through
> redemption that is in Christ Jesus. (Rom. 3:23)

Terminology of the Secret Doctrine

The terminology of the secret doctrine of the Masonic lodge is largely unfamiliar to Christians and, for that matter, many Masons. General categories of terms describe major concepts. Often multiple terms are used to refer to a particular concept. Cosmic consciousness, Christ-consciousness, and possession of the lost word all refer to the same state, the Christ-state, wherein the individual Mason has worked out his own salvation. Initiation, Evolution, Divine Science, Science of Soul Development, and Soul Architecture, are terms that all describe the same salvation process.

In the secret doctrine, possession of the lost word is the key to salvation. In *The Mysticism of Masonry*, Clymer writes: "After the candidate is obligated and brought to Light in the third degree, he is bantered with the statement that undoubtedly he now imagines himself a Master Mason. He is informed not only that such is not the case but that there is no certainty that he will ever become such. He subsequently starts on his journey for the discovery of the Lost Word."[27]

Clymer is referring here to that section of the third degree ritual just prior to the portion where the candidate portrays Hiram Abiff. The candidate is intentionally misled that the lodge is about to be closed. He is asked how it feels to be a Master Mason, etc., and then the Worshipful Master tells him, "Brother [man's name], you are not yet a Master Mason, neither do I know that you will ever be . . ."

The hoodwink is again placed over his eyes before the ritual continues. The candidate then portrays Hiram Abiff in the Legend of the Third Degree, which deals with the death of Hiram and the loss of the word. Clymer writes of the lost word,

Every man who takes upon himself the Masonic
obligation, can, if he will, find this Lost Word. The
material required in the process of transmutation
is within himself as surely as a man who has his
cellar filled with coal and a furnace wherein to
burn it, has all that is required to start a roaring
fire which will heat his house. Finding the Lost
Word is an individual work. Each Soul must accomplish it or miss Immortality and this is true
whether a man be a churchman or a Mason or
both. (55)

In the last sentence, Clymer claims that churchmen,
those who have accepted Jesus as their Lord and Savior
and who have faith in Jesus as the Christ, will not have
salvation unless they also find the lost word.

Other Masonic writers stress the importance of finding the lost word. Consider the words of Rev. Charles H.
Vail in *Ancient Mysteries and Modern Masonry*: "The symbol
of the Lost Word and the legend of the search for it,
embodies the whole design of Freemasonry. The primary
object of Freemasonry is the search after Divine Truth.
The Word is a symbol of this Divine Truth, and this truth
is the key to the Science of the Soul."[28] Vail reveals clearly
that the lost word is not a literal word but a symbol that
represents divine truth. Masonic writer Manly Palmer Hall
wrote *The Lost Keys of Freemasonry*. Hall was lifted up as
Masonry's greatest philosopher in his obituary in the
November 1990 issue of the *Scottish Rite Journal*. Although
Hall wrote more than fifty books and sixty-five smaller
works, *The Lost Keys of Freemasonry* is the most well known
and used. The obituary stated, "Hall did not teach a new
doctrine but was an ambassador of an ageless tradition of
wisdom that enriches us to this day."[29]

Hall wrote of the lost word in his work, *The Lost Keys
of Freemasonry*: "The Word is found when the Master himself is ordained by the living hand of God, cleansed by
living water, baptized by living fire, a Priest King after the
Order of Melchizedek who is above the law."[30]

Hall is saying that the Master Mason becomes a Christ when the lost word is found. The Melchizedek priesthood is the priesthood of Jesus Christ mentioned in Hebrews 5:5-6. The teaching that man can become a Christ is the cornerstone of the secret doctrine. Masonry's greatest philosopher embraced that teaching until his death in 1990.

In *Ancient Operative Masonry*, S.R. Parchment sums up Masonic teaching on the lost word, the Christ within, and redemption contained in the secret doctrine:

> The "Lost Word" is the Christ within, to which the Mystic Mason looks for redemption. Thus the Master Jesus, who was an Initiate of the Ancient Operative School, taught his followers that the kingdom of heaven is within. In the early church, as in the secret doctrine, there was not a personal Christ for the whole world but a potential Christ in every living being. Yea, the mystic while investigating the intangible realms beholds potential Christs in the atoms which compose the universe. Hence Masons believe in the Architect of the Universe, but positively not in Jesus the man as the only Son of God. (S. R. Parchment, *Ancient Operative Masonry* [San Francisco, CA: W. B. Conley Co., 1930], 35)

Discovering the Lost Word

The process through which the lost word is rediscovered is known as Initiation. Initiation, Evolution, Divine Science, Science of Soul Development, Soul Architecture, and rediscovery of the lost word are all important terms in the language of the secret doctrine, and all describe the salvation process. Understanding the secret doctrine requires understanding Masonic Initiation.

The Significance of Initiation

H. L. Haywood wrote about the significance of Initiation in the chapter titled "The Meaning of Initiation and Secrecy" in *The Great Teachings of Masonry*: "Masonic initiation is intended to be quite as profound and as revolutionizing an experience. As result of it the candidate should become a new man: he should have a new range of thought; a new feeling about mankind; a new idea about God."[31]

After the reader has become fully aware of the secret doctrine, the statement will be understood to have a ponderous meaning. In the chapter titled "The Secret Doctrine Continued," in Buck's book *Mystic Masonry,* we find that the process of human evolution (Initiation) is one in which man evolves from man into God by becoming Christ.

> Becoming perfect in Humanity, man attains Divinity. In other words, he becomes Christos. This is the meaning, aim, and consummation of Human Evolution; and this Philosophy defines the one-only process by which it may be attained. The Perfect Man is Christ: and Christ is God. This is the birth-right and destiny of every human soul. (85-6)

Initiation is the evolutionary process by which the secret doctrine declares that man can become a Christ and, therefore, God. This is the same deception that Satan used with Eve.

The Technique of Initiation

Those unacquainted with the secret doctrine would initially assume that Initiation is a ceremony, but such an assumption is incorrect. *Mystic Masonry* by Buck contains an explanation: "All real Initiation is an internal, not an external process. . . . It is thus that man must 'work out his own salvation.' The consummation of initiation is the Perfect Master, the Christos, for these are the same. They are the goal, the perfect consummation of human evolution."[32]

This provides a clue to the true nature of Initiation. Initiation does not refer to a ceremony, but to an internal process. The discipline of Initiation is discussed in great detail in *The Masonic Initiation* by W. L. Wilmshurst:

It may be a surprise to some members of our Craft to be told that our ceremonial rites, as at present performed, do not constitute or confer real Initiation at all, in the original sense of admitting a man to the solemn mysteries of the human soul, and to practical experience in divine science. . . . We profess to confer Initiation, but few Masons know what real Initiation involves; very few, one fears, would have the wish, the courage, or the willingness to make the necessary sacrifices to attain it if they did. (W. L. Wilmshurst, *The Masonic Initiation* [London: Percy Lund Humphries and Co. Limited, 1924], 17)

The meaning of the last sentence in this last quotation is profound. What kind of sacrifices are required? Wilmshurst's statement that few Masons know what real Initiation involves is true. His suggestion that very few would be willing to make the required sacrifice if they did understand is also true. Wilmshurst continues:

For real Initiation means an expansion of consciousness from the human to the divine level. (19)

For those upon the path to real Initiation, meditation is essential. (45)

Initiation always occurs when the physical body is in a state of trance or sleep, and when the temporarily liberated consciousness has been transferred to a higher level. . . . Yet in the actual experience of soul-architecture Initiation succeeds Initiation upon increasingly higher levels of the ladder as the individual becomes correspondingly ripe for them, able to bear their strain and to assimilate their revelations. (87–8)

Initiation has no other end than this: conscious union between the individual soul and the Universal Divine Spirit. (54)

So then, Initiation is a process in which a Mason goes into a trance by passive meditation and attains conscious union; that is, he establishes communications with the Masonic god. By attaining conscious union with that god, he becomes a Christ. The process of Initiation recurs over months and years, and, after each conscious union with the Masonic god, he has new understandings about himself and about the god. Initiation is evolutionary; the Mason evolves into a god himself.

Identifying the God of Freemasonry

Clearly, Masons who discover the lost word through the process of Initiation do not attain conscious union with their god through Jesus. They deny that Jesus is the one true Christ. From the writings of John, we can be certain that the God of the Bible is not the Masonic god: "Who is a liar but he that denieth that Jesus is the Christ? He is antichrist, that denieth the Father and the Son. Whosoever denieth the Son, the same hath not the Father: [but] he that acknowledgeth the Son hath the Father also" (1 John 2:22–3). John tells us that he that denies that Jesus is the Christ is antichrist. And, Paul tells us that there is only one God and one Christ: "But to us there is but one God, the Father, of whom are all things, and we in him; and one Lord Jesus Christ, by whom are all things, and we by him" (1 Cor. 8:6).

The secret doctrine teaches that Jesus was born an ordinary man and that He became a Christ later. He did not come as Christ in the flesh. *The Meaning of Masonry*, by Lynn Perkins contains the following: "Jesus of Nazareth had attained a level of consciousness, of perfection, that has been called by various names: cosmic consciousness, soul regeneration, philosophic initiation, spiritual illumination, Brahmic Splendor, Christ-consciousness."[33] Perkins writes that Jesus attained Christ-consciousness. Perkins is saying that Jesus did not have Christ-consciousness, which is the same thing as the consciousness of Christ, when He came in the flesh. We know from the writings of John, therefore, that *the god of Freemasonry is the spirit of antichrist*:

> And every spirit that confesseth not that Jesus
> Christ is come in the flesh is not of God: and this
> is that spirit of antichrist, whereof ye have heard
> that it should come; and even now already is it in
> the world. (1 John 4:3)

> For many deceivers are entered into the world,
> who confess not that Jesus Christ is come in the
> flesh. This is a deceiver and an antichrist. (2 John
> 1:7)

Conscious Union with the Spirit of Antichrist

Masons who embrace the secret doctrine attain conscious union with the spirit of antichrist. Manly Palmer Hall offers some clues in *The Lost Keys of Freemasonry*: "When the Mason learns that the key to the warrior on the block is the proper application of the dynamo of living power, he has learned the mystery of his Craft. The seething energies of Lucifer are in his hands and before he may step onward and upward, he must prove his ability to properly apply energy."[34]

Hall, Freemasonry's greatest philosopher, indicates that Lucifer is the power behind the lodge and that those who learn the mysteries of the craft may tap into the seething energies of Lucifer. Hall also identifies the spirit that Masons attain union with in words which most Masons do not understand:

> In Freemasonry is concealed the mystery of creation, the answer to the problem of existence, and
> the path the student must tread in order to join
> those who are really the living powers behind the
> thrones of modern national and international affairs. (18)

> The Master Mason, if he be truly a Master, is in
> communication with the unseen powers that move
> the destinies of life. (57)

What does the Bible say? Who is this unseen power which controls the world? "We know that we are children of God, and that the whole world is under the control of the evil one" (1 John 5:19, NIV).

The Builders was written by Joseph Fort Newton in 1914. It is the classic that today is often presented to newly raised Master Masons. The bibliography contains references to most of the major books and authors that reveal the hidden meanings behind Masonry. In the chapter titled "Secret Doctrine," the following is found: "Perhaps the greatest student in this field of esoteric teaching and method, certainly the greatest now living, is Arthur Edward Waite, to whom it is a pleasure to pay tribute."[35] The tribute continues from page fifty-seven through page sixty-one. Newton speaks of Waite's writings as "a series of volumes noble in form, united in aim, unique in wealth of revealing beauty, and of unequaled worth."[36]

Waite, who until his death in 1945 was considered a great student of the secret doctrine, wrote such books as *Devil Worship in France, The Book of Black Magic,* and *The Way of Divine Union.* On pages 244 through 248 of *The Book of Black Magic* are detailed instructions for conjuring "Emperor Lucifer, master and prince of rebellious spirits."[37] For obvious reasons it will not be quoted here. One of the Masonic greats, Waite, was a Luciferian.

Scriptural Evidence of Demonic Communication

Is conscious union with the spirit of antichrist or communication with demons possible? Consider Paul's words to Timothy: "Now the Spirit speaketh expressly, that in the latter times some shall depart from the faith, giving heed to seducing spirits, and doctrines of devils; Speaking lies in hypocrisy; having their conscience seared with a hot iron" (1 Tim. 4:1-2).

It is obvious that for anyone to give heed to seducing spirits and their doctrines, the doctrines must be communicated from the seducing spirits to man. The Masonic doctrine that a Mason can become a Christ is not of God. It is clearly of Satan, the Antichrist. Masonic Initiation is a process, central to the secret doctrine, whereby the doctrines of devils are communicated to Masons by demons while they are in trance. The previously quoted passage from *The Masonic Initiation* can be understood to agree with the realities as predicted in Scripture: "Yet in the actual experience of soul-architecture Initiation succeeds Initiation upon increasingly higher levels of the ladder as the individual becomes correspondingly ripe for them, able to bear their strain and to assimilate their revelations."[38]

The process of Masonic Initiation is one in which the conscience of the individual is seared as with a hot iron. As his spirit is progressively deadened, he is able to bear more, and then more, of the revelations of darkness.

The Expected Result of Masonic Initiation

Knowing the identity of the Masonic god, a clear understanding of the result of conscious union with that god becomes possible. From *Ancient Mysteries and Modern Masonry*, we learn that "Initiation, as we shall see in a subsequent lecture, was regeneration-a real spiritual 'new becoming' or re-birth. The candidate himself became the thing symbolized-Hermes, Buddha, Christ, etc. This state was the result of real Initiation—an evolution of the human into the divine."[39]

He is saying that a Masonic initiate is reborn and has a new becoming. When a man becomes a Christian, he is reborn. Masonry has a similar born-again experience that will literally change a man's life. From *The Masonic Initiation*:

> True self-knowledge is unobstructed conscious union of the human spirit with God and the realization of their identity. In that identic union the unreal, superficial selves have become obliterated. The sense of personality is lost, merged in the Impersonal and Universal. The little Ego is assumed into the great All, and knows as It knows. Man realizes his own inherent ultimate Divinity, and thenceforth lives and acts no longer as a separate individual, with an independent will, but in integration with the Divine Life and Will, whose instrument he becomes, whose purposes he thenceforth serves. (page 49)

The Mason becomes unable to act as a separate individual and becomes an instrument of the Masonic god. In *Ancient Mysteries and Modern Masonry*, Rev. Charles H. Vail writes, "The consummation of all this was to make the Initiate a God, either by union with a Divine Being without or by the realization of the Divine Self within."[40]

With a clear understanding of the secret doctrine, we can understand the true meaning of the following passages that were quoted previously. From the chapter titled "The Meaning of Initiation and Secrecy" in *The Great Teachings of Masonry*, we read that "Masonic initiation is intended to be quite as profound and revolutionizing an experience. As a result of it the candidate should become a new man: he should have a new range of thought; a new feeling about mankind; a new idea about God. . . ."[41]

The statement from *The Masonic Initiation* by W. L. Wilmshurst also can be seen to have a profound meaning: "We profess to confer Initiation, but few Masons know what real Initiation involves; very few, one fears, would have the wish, the courage, or the willingness to make the necessary sacrifices to attain it if they did."[42]

Understanding the Purpose of the Masonic Lodge

In *The Great Teachings of Masonry*. H. L. Haywood wrote, "The Fraternity itself exists in order to keep fixed on a man a certain set of influences, and in order to bring about certain changes in the world, etc.: its secrecy is a means to that end, and helps to make such a purpose possible."[43] It is clear from an understanding of the secret doctrine and of Scripture, the certain set of influences Haywood is referring to are demons. Haywood reveals the reason for Masonic secrecy. In *The Masonic Initiation*, we can see that the objective of Masonry is to bring men under the influence of demons through the process of Masonic Initiation: "Initiation has no other end than this-conscious union between the individual soul and the Universal Divine Spirit."[44] Wilmshurst continues, saying that "The whole purpose and end of Initiation-the union of the personal soul with its Divine Principle. Masonry has no other objective than this; all other matters of interest connected with it are but details subsidiary to this supreme achievement."[45]

Summary

The following is a summary of the major teachings contained in the secret doctrine:

1. There is not one Christ for the whole world, but a potential Christ in each man. It is far more important to become a Christ than it is to believe that Jesus was Christ.

2. Since each man can become a Christ himself, Masons have no need for the cleansing blood of Jesus.

3. Through the process of Masonic Initiation, man may attain conscious union with the god of Freemasonry. The process of Masonic Initiation is not a ceremony, but an internal process that occurs while the individual is in trance.

4. When conscious union with the Masonic god is attained, the lost word is found. The Mason has worked out his own salvation. He has become a Christ and thus a god himself.

But, that is just not so. Jesus said it as simply as it could be stated, "I am the way, and the truth, and the life. No one comes to the Father except through me" (John 14:6).

Endnotes

1. *Coil's Masonic Encyclopedia*, s.v. "Rituals."

2. Lawrence R. Taylor *Indiana Monitor and Freemason's Guide* (Grand Lodge of Indiana, 1959, 1975), 37-8.

3. *Coil's Masonic Encyclopedia*, s.v. "Charter."

4. *Indiana Monitor*, 23.

5. *Indiana Blue Book of Masonic Law* (Grand Lodge Free and Accepted Masons of the State of Indiana, 1953), 75.

6. *Indiana Monitor*, 35.

7. Ibid.

8. *Masonic Manual and Code* (Atlanta, GA: Grand Lodge of Free and Accepted Masons of Georgia, 1944), 313.

9. Ibid., 315.

10. *Masonic Text Book*, 19th ed. (The Grand Lodge of A. F. & A. M. of the state of West Virginia, 1919), 25.

11. Ibid.

12. *Indiana Monitor*, 11.

13. H. L. Haywood, *The Great Teachings of Masonry* (Richmond, VA: Macoy Publishing, 1986), 33.

14. *Indiana Monitor*, 38.

15. Albert G. Mackey, *Manual of the Lodge* (New York, NY: Macoy and Sickles, 1862), 96.

16. Ibid., 96.

17. *Masonic Manual of Alabama* (Alabama, GA: Grand Lodge F. & A. M. of Alabama, 1913), 42, 78, 79.

Florida Masonic Monitor (Jacksonville, FL: Grand Lodge F. & A. M. of Florida, 1977), 39, 109–10.

Masonic Manual and Code (Atlanta, GA: Grand Lodge F. & A. M. of Georgia, 1944), 22, 70.

Idaho Monitor (Grand Lodge of A. F. & A. M. of the state of Idaho, 1903), 11, 53.

The Official Monitor of the Most Worshipful Grand Lodge Ancient Free and Accepted Masons (Illinois: Grand Lodge of Illinois, 1962), 24, 66.

Indiana Monitor and Freemason's Guide, 63–4, 101–3.

William M. Shaver, *Shaver's Masonic Monitor* (Topeka, KS: Wm. M. Shaver and A. K. Wilson Publishers, 1899), 37, 103.

Henry Pirtle, *The Kentucky Monitor* (Louisville, Kentucky: Standard Printing Co., 1946), 41, 145.

Michigan Monitor and Ceremonies (Grand Lodge F. & A. M., Michigan, 1918), 10, 39. Masonic Manual and *Monitorial Instructions of the Grand Lodge of A. F. & A. M. of Minnesota* (Grand Lodge of Minnesota, 1964), 21, 53.

Blue Lodge Text-Book (Grand Lodge of Mississippi Free and Accepted Masons, 1978), 15, 44.

Monitor and Ceremonies, Ancient, Free, and Accepted Masons (Grand Lodge of Nebraska, 1923), 25, 65.

North Carolina Lodge Manual (Grand Lodge of Ancient, Free and Accepted Masons of North Carolina, 1979), 25, 65.

Manual of Dayton Lodge No. 147 (Dayton, Ohio: Groneweg Printing Co., 1921), 68, 90.

Manual of Miami Valley Lodge No. 660 (Dayton, Ohio: Free and Accepted Masons, 1921), 29, 51.

Ahiman Rezon (Columbia, South Carolina: Grand Lodge of Ancient Free Masons of South Carolina, 1947), 90, 155.

Tennessee Craftsman or *Masonic Textbook* (Grand Lodge F. and A. M., 1972), 22, 95.

Wm. M. Taylor, *A Manual of Freemasonry adapted to the Work and Government of the Lodges Subordinate to the Grand Lodge of Texas* (Houston, TX: W.H. Coyle Printer & Publisher, 1883), 29, 81.

Virginia Text Book (Highland springs, VA: Grand Lodge, Free and Accepted Masons of Virginia, 1944), 94, 122, 123.

Masonic Text Book for Use of the Lodges in West Virginia (Most Worshipful Grand Lodge of A. F. & A. M. of the State of West Virginia, 1919), 41, 84-5.

18. *Indiana Monitor*, 124.

19. Joseph Fort Newton, *The Builders* (Richmond, VA: Macoy Publishing, 1951).

20. *Indiana Monitor*, 20.

21. Henry Pirtle, ed., *Kentucky Monitor*, 8th edition (Louisville, KY: The Standard Printing Co., 1946), ix.

22. Ibid., xix.

23. R. Swinburne Clymer, *The Mysticism of Masonry* (Quakertown, Pennsylvania: The Philosophical Publishing Company, 1924), 48.

24. George Steinmetz, *The Lost Word Its Hidden Meaning* (New York, NY: Macoy Masonic Publishing, 1953).

25. Indiana Monitor, 144-5.

26. *Kentucky Monitor*, xvi.

27. R. Swinburne Clymer, *The Mysticism of Masonry*, 49.

28. Rev. Charles H. Vail, *Ancient Mysteries and Modern Masonry* (New York, NY: Macoy Publishing, 1909), 211.

29. *Scottish Rite Journal* (November 1990): 22

30. Manly Palmer Hall, *The Lost Keys of Freemasonry* (Richmond, VA: Macoy Publishing, 1923), 59.

31. H. L. Haywood, *The Great Teachings of Masonry*, 31.

32. J. D. Buck, *Mystic Masonry*, 86.

33. Lynn F. Perkins, *The Meaning of Masonry* (Lakemont, GA: CSA Press, 1971), 53.

34. Manly Palmer Hall, *The Lost Keys of Freemasonry*, 48.

35. Joseph Fort Newton, *The Builders*, 57.

36. Ibid., 59.

37. Arthur Edward Waite, The Book of Black Magic (York Beach, Maine: first American Printing in 1972 by Samuel Weiser, Inc., 1989).

38. W. L. Wilmshurst, *The Masonic Initiation*, 87–8.

39. Rev. Charles H. Vail, *Ancient Mysteries and Modern Masonry*, 33.

40. Ibid., 25.

41. H. L. Haywood, *The Great Teachings of Masonry*, 31.

42. W. L. Wilmshurst, *The Masonic Initiation*, 17.

43. H. L. Haywood, *The Great Teachings of Masonry*, 33.

44. W. L. Wilmshurst, *The Masonic Initiation*, 54.

45. Ibid., 55.

Seven

Freemasonry: The Witchcraft Connection

William J. Schnoebelen

William Schnoebelen was deeply involved in both witchcraft, as a Wiccan high priest, and the Masonic Order for many years. He was a Mason for nine years and a witch for sixteen years. In the lodge, he held offices of Junior Warden in the Blue Lodge, Prelate in the Commandery of the York Rite, Master of the Veil in the Royal Arch Degree, and Associate Patron in the order of the Eastern Star. Additionally, he was a Thirty-second Degree Mason and a Shriner. He is now a born-again Christian and the author of five books, including *Masonry: Beyond the Light*.

"For rebellion is as the sin of witchcraft, and stubbornness is as iniquity and idolatry" (1 Sam. 15:23).

In understanding the spiritual difficulties of a born-again Christian being a Mason, it is necessary to realize that there are highly occult elements woven into the very warp and woof of Freemasonry. Thus, the lodge is not just another religion like the Muslims or the Buddhists—although that alone should be enough to keep Christians from involving themselves in it. The nature and character of the lodge's deepest theological underpinnings are rooted in witchcraft and paganism.

Now that may be an astonishing assertion to some, especially to most Masons. However, it is very easily proven. Few people, within the craft of Masonry or otherwise, perceive that just because a Bible lies open on the altar and Bible verses and characters play an important part in the ritual of the lodge, that this does not prevent the lodge from being of the nature of the occult or witchcraft.

This can be illustrated by a very simple illustration. Back in the 1970s, when I first became a witch, a very popular how-to book on magic was Raymond Buckland's *Popular Candle-Burning*.[1] In this book were "recipes" for spells for everything from healing, to love spells, to protection spells. On one set of pages of the book would be a spell for healing, complete with instructions on the burning and movement of certain colored candles. The spell would be a full-blown witchcraft ritual, pagan to the core!

On the following pages would be the same ritual, with the same candles, the same instructions. However, the text of the "spell" would be drawn from the Psalms or other Bible verses. These were provided for readers who were a little too squeamish to actually do a witchcraft incantation, but still wanted results.

Now the question becomes: Even though those rituals were full of psalms, were they still witchcraft? Of course, the answer would have to be yes. In like manner, even though Bible phrases and characters abound in the Masonic ritual work, the presence of those elements cannot somehow "sanctify" what is essentially a pagan ritual full of witchcraft overtones.

Defining Terms

Perhaps it would be helpful to have a few terms defined before we go further. Witchcraft (or Wicca,[2] the term for "white" or good witchcraft) can be broadly defined as a mystery religion based on the ancient fertility cults of pre-Christian Europe. Many witches are polytheists—meaning that they believe in more than one god or goddess. Some are monotheists, believing in only one deity. Even most polytheistic witches today, however, acknowledge that ultimately there is one supreme deity somewhere. The popular saying by twentieth century master occultist Dion Fortune (Violet Firth) speaks to this: "All Gods are one God, all Goddesses are one Goddess, and there is but one Initiator." Pressed, you will find that most knowledgeable witches will reveal that the "one Initiator" is Lucifer, who is the Light-Bringer, the Illuminator, and the sun-deity. He is not felt to be a devil-figure by Wiccans, but only the consort of the Great Mother Goddess.

Witchcraft, in its religious sense, involves the veneration of the forces of reproduction—both in plant, animal, and human life. Thus, human and animal sexuality are revered, the cycle of the seasons celebrated, and rituals do frequently involve the use of ritual tools that symbolize the human reproductive organs (wands, daggers, goblets, cauldrons, etc.) Many witchcraft groups even have ritual sex, believing that this is an important way to encounter the gods.

The term *mystery religion* means that it is a religion in which elements are kept hidden from the "profane" (nonmembers). You can only learn these elements by going through a formal initiation in which you are ceremonially set apart from the masses and sworn formally to secrecy. Only then are you entrusted with the group's secrets, and then in degrees. In other words, there are things a "third grade" or "third degree" witch is allowed to know that a first degree witch is not.

A secondary element in witchcraft is the belief in magic. However, it is *only* secondary—contrary to popular belief. A good—though broad—definition of magic that many witches would accept is that given by magician (and Thirty-third Degree Mason) Aleister Crowley: "the art and science of causing change to occur in conformity with

[your] will." Though this definition is broad enough to
include things normally not thought of as magic like picking up a pencil (you caused a change in the pencil's
position to occur in conformity with your will), most
witches understand it to mainly apply to causing change
to occur without a visible, tangible cause in the environ-
ment.

Many witches do not attempt to "work magic" (in the
sense of trying to cause change to occur in the forces of
nature or human beings) but just enjoy worshipping their
gods or goddesses. Thus, it is not an absolute requirement that witches practice magic or that a magician be a
witch. In fact, the above-mentioned Aleister Crowley would
never have called himself a witch (or warlock).[3]

Finally, we need to define paganism. This is basically
a belief in the forces of nature as being sacred. Pagans are
usually pantheists in that they believe that a kind of god-
force is in everything—trees, animals, rocks, etc. Essentially, a pagan believes most everything the witch believes,
but is kind of a lay person, whereas a witch is more of a
priestess or shaman. The typical pagan may not have
access to some of the deeper "mysteries" of witchcraft,
which are not available to the uninitiated.

Getting Down to Business: Ritual Resemblances

With these definitions in mind, we can begin to examine the similarities between the Masonic theology and
ritual and the workings of a witchcraft group. One point,
however, must be clarified. Modern Wicca is just that—
modern. Although it claims mythic descent to groups
back in the Stone Age, it is actually a comparatively modern
religion. As it is currently constituted, Wicca is barely a
century old. This is not to say that it doesn't draw on
elements from the ancient mystery cults. To be certain, it
does—to a high degree. However, it is a difficult task to
ascertain whether contemporary Wicca so strongly resembles Freemasonry because two of its principle archi-
tects (Aleister Crowley and Gerald B. Gardner) were
Masons; or whether that similarity is a derivation of more
ancient practices.

As interesting an academic point as that might be, it is essentially irrelevant to the broader question. If Masonic rituals were engrafted into witchcraft in the late nineteenth and early twentieth century and if that melding was so seamless and effortless—even to the point that, in some cases, the Wiccan rites were less bizarre and blasphemous than their Masonic counterpart—then what message does that send about Masonry? As a preacher friend of mine, Jim Spencer, observed, "If the devil can preach my sermons without changing them much, what does that say about my sermons?"

With that point in mind, let us look first at the ritual similarities between contemporary Wicca and Freemasonry:

A. Both are built on a foundational system of three degrees, with a few forms of Wicca offering some higher degrees after the third degree has been achieved.

B. Both are secret societies in that both membership rolls are secret, and secrets are kept from the general populace (to a greater or lesser degree) by both religions. Both generally meet in secret, except for rare open and public events.

C. Both have highly ceremonial initiations to pass from one degree to another, including sworn oaths.

D. Both have ceremonial purgings and purifications of their ritual space before commencing any ritual work.

E. The precise similarities between the two groups are that both groups

    1. Cause candidates to strip off all secular clothing;

    2. Cause the candidate to be divested of all metal;

    3. Hoodwink (blindfold) the candidate and ceremonially tie ropes around him (though the form of the tying varies);

    4. Cause the candidate to stand in the Northeast corner of the "temple"[4] in the first degree;

    5. Challenge the candidate by piercing their naked chest with a sharp instrument (witches use a sword, Masons, the point of a compass);

    6. Challenge the candidate with secret passwords;

7. Lead the candidate blindfolded in a circum-
ambulation (walking around) of the temple; and

8. Require the candidate to swear solemn oaths of
secrecy before being given custody of the secrets of
the group.

Interestingly enough, the oaths of a witch are much
milder and less gruesome than the oaths of a Freemason.
Here is the text of a first grade oath from the witchcraft
Book of Shadows (ritual workbook):

> I, [NAME], in the presence of the Mighty Ones, do
> of my own free will and accord, most solemnly
> swear that I will ever keep the secrets of the Arte
> [*Magical Arts*—author] and never reveal the secrets
> of the Arte, except it be to a proper person, prop-
> erly prepared and within a magic circle such as I
> am now in. . . .
>
> All this I swear, by all my hopes of a future life,
> mindful that my measure has been taken; and may
> my weapons turn against me, if I should break
> this, my solemn oath.[5]

This sounds ridiculously mild in comparison to the
first degree oath of an Entered Apprentice Mason, which
is too long to quote in its entirety, but that ends like this:

> All this I most solemnly and sincerely promise and
> swear, with a firm and steadfast resolution to keep
> and perform the same binding myself under no
> less penalty than that of having my throat cut across,
> my tongue torn out by its roots, and my body
> buried in the rough sands of the sea, at low water
> mark, where the tide ebbs and flows twice in twenty-
> four hours, should I ever knowingly violate this my
> Entered Apprentice obligation, so help me God
> and keep me steadfast in the due performance of
> the same. (Malcolm C. Duncan's Ritual Monitor
> [New York: David McKay Co., Inc.], 34–5)

As all students of Freemasonry know, that grisly oath
is but the beginning in a series of ever more horrid oaths

that the candidate is required to take. The oaths of the three degrees of witchcraft are like a Sunday school lesson by comparison! But, let's return to our list of similarities:

9. Both have a ceremonial unhoodwinking of the candidate, following the oath, before lighted candles that is intended to bring "illumination."

10. Both convey to the new initiate the "working tools" pertinent to that degree, and each of their uses are taught to them.

11. In both, the tools have correspondences both in the ceremonial realm and in similarities to human reproduction.

12. Both, in the higher degrees, take the initiate through a ritual death-and-rebirth experience in which the initiate acts the part of a hero (heroine) of the craft.

13. Both cause the candidate to endure (while being blindfolded) being picked up, spun around, carried around, being jostled or struck from person to person. This is supposed to produce an "altered state of consciousness."

14. Both Wicca and Freemasonry are, by coincidence or design, both referred to as "The Craft."

Philosophical Similarities

Having given almost two dozen precise similarities between the ritual work of witchcraft and the lodge, it should not surprise us to see that there is also some doctrinal, or philosophical, resemblance between the two.

Both witches and Masons revere the powers of human reproduction (albeit most Masons do so unknowingly). The most obvious example of this is the use of the ceremonial Masonic apron, which covers the "Holy of Holies" of Freemasonry, the male groin area. This fact has been adequately documented in many places.[6]

The authorities of Freemasonry, most notably Albert Pike, Thirty-third Degree, and Manly P. Hall, Thirty-third Degree (both occultists par excellence) write that the essential, underlying philosophy of Freemasonry is Kabbalism and Gnosticism.[7] Kabbalism is a system of Jewish mysticism and magic and is the foundational element in modern witchcraft. Virtually all of the great witches and sorcerers of this century were Kabbalists. Gnosticism is an ancient, anti-Christian heresy best summarized by the statement "One is saved by acquiring secret, unknown knowledge [Greek: gnosis]." Thus, all mystery religions, including witchcraft and Masonry are, per force, Gnostic in character.

Both witches and Freemasons seek salvation through "illumination" or receiving "The Light." This is important because of the centrality of this symbolism in both sects.

Both groups teach a kind of salvation by works, not grace.[8] The occult doctrine of reincarnation is explicitly taught in witchcraft and implicitly taught in the lodge.

Finally, both groups deny the unique character and mission of the Lord Jesus Christ.[9] Both deny the resurrection of Christ.[10] Most people would have no trouble believing that witches deny these beliefs, but in this, the Wicca are identical to the theology of the lodge.

Getting to the Root

There are also significant historical antecedents that go a long way towards explaining this current "coziness" between witchcraft and Masonry. It can be readily shown that Freemasonry is rooted in the medieval occult societies of Europe, such as the Templars and the Rosicrucians.[11]

Indeed, many Masonic writers boast about these connections. Additional associations pop up with the dangerously subversive Illuminati Ordnen of Adam Weishaupt in the eighteenth century.[12]

It is vital to understand that this past interchange between Masonry and these various occult groups did not stop in the eighteenth century. If anything, it has grown more prominent in the past century. There is something about the lodge that has always attracted sorcerers. The historical list of occultists and witches in the last century who were Freemasons reads like a *Who's Who* of twentieth century occultism:

• Arthur Edward Waite—occult writer and Masonic historian.

• Dr. Wynn Westcott—member of the Societas Rosicruciana in Anglia and founding member of the occult Order of the Golden Dawn—the most influential magical society of the nineteenth to early twentieth century.

• S. L. MacGregor Mathers—cofounder of the Golden Dawn.

• Aleister Crowley—master Satanist of this century and founder of the antichrist religion of Thelema—claimed to be "The Great Beast 666."

• Dr. Gerard Encauss—(Papus) masterful author, teacher of the Tarot and leader of the occult Martiniste society.

• Dr. Theodore Reuss—head of the O.T.O., a German occult/satanic society which made Crowley its head for the British Isles.

• George Pickingill—the Grand Master witch of nineteenth century England, leader of the "Pickingill covens."

• Annie Besant—leader of the occult Theosophical society and Co-Masonic hierarch (Yes, there are female Masons!).[13]

• Alice Bailey—founder of the proto-New Age organization, Lucis (formerly Lucifer) Trust.

• Bishop Charles W. Leadbetter—Theosophist, mentor to the failed New Age "Christ," Krishnamurti, and prelate in the occult Liberal Catholic Church.

• Manly P. Hall—Rosicrucian adept, author, founder of the Philosophical Research Society.

• Gerald B. Gardner—founder of the modern Wiccan (white witchcraft) revival.

• Alex Sanders—self-styled "King of the Witches" in London and one of the most influential leaders of Wicca after Gardner.

Would you really wish to belong to an organization that welcomed these powerful sorcerers into its midst with open arms? This is not to mention the many minor occultists (as I was) who are in the lodge—drawn by its mysterious power. At least three or four of my male witch friends were in the Masons, and all of my leaders were! There is a real reason for this strong affinity between Masonry and witchcraft. It is because the lodge is plugged into an international network of witchcraft—a hierarchy of evil.

The "All-Seeing Eye" of the Masons is, of course, an occult symbol.[14] Its use on the Great Seal of the United States is not without significance either. (See the back of any dollar bill.) You will note that the "Eye" is there perched atop an incomplete pyramid with the date (in Roman numerals) of 1776 A.D. at the bottom.

The year 1776 is also the year that Adam Weishaupt founded the Illuminati! Then, realize that the trapezoid (what the unfinished pyramid really is) is a most significant symbol in Satanism.[15] The symbol on that seal is actually a metaphor for the oppressive hierarchy which reigns over the Masonic lodge, and by extension, over much of U.S. government, and the "Eye" symbolizes Lucifer's dominion over it.

Being a Mason (of whatever degree) is like going through your life with all that spiritual garbage weighing down on you. It is like having a King Kong-sized monkey on your back! While all levels of Masonry have their share of witches, the Palladium, the Illuminati, the Ancient rites, and the Supreme Council are especially likely to have them, in one form or another.

The Mason is "unequally yoked" together with all these unbelievers and witches in rebellion to the Word of God (2 Cor. 6:14-8) and that alone is enough to knock the spiritual stuffing out of any man, even supposedly "good, solid Christians!"

You see, in an occult sense, Freemasonry is much like the fabled "pyramid scheme." It is a hierarchy in which the highest levels leech off the lower levels. Just as in the marketing schemes, the person at the top of the pyramid draws in most of the revenues because of the efforts of hundreds or thousands of people under him, so the same element works within the lodge, even as it does—to a much smaller degree—in a witchcraft coven!

First of all, it is a financial pyramid. We have already mentioned that a Mason must spend hundreds of dollars, perhaps close to a thousand, to go through the degrees. Additionally, they must pay dues every year to each and every body they have joined. This could amount, depending on the level of involvement, to several hundred dollars a year.

While some of that money goes into necessities, and some of it goes into charity, some of it also ends up in places of which lodge members have no knowledge. Of course, our local leaders were obviously not getting rich, but there was a lot of free-floating cash somewhere up in the ranks.

"Psychic Vampires" in the Leadership?

In the occult, we used to talk about psychic vampires—people who just seemed to suck the life out of a person. Of course, black magicians excel in this. They leave people feeling drained. What most people don't realize is that an organization can function in much the same way.

The lodge functions like a spiritual sponge in many ways. Think of all the millions of man-hours Masons put into their lodge work: memorizing the degree material, attendance at meetings, extracurricular lodge activities (dinners, banquets, funerals, picnics). Those Masons who are Christians pour hours of time and energy into the lodge, and it just laps it up and begs for more. I know, I used to be heavily involved in lodge work. I was out of the house at least two week nights! Then, because I was a lodge officer, I had to spend additional hours working on memorizing the ritual work. I had to be there before the lodge opened and after it closed. I had to attend all lodge functions and funerals.

Think of the lodge meeting itself: it is opened in solemn fashion, with a ritual which may take fifteen to twenty minutes. If there is an initiation, the meeting can run to hours, sometimes three or four hours for third degree. All that energy is going somewhere, friends, and it isn't to God!

I can only speak from witchcraft experience, but quite often our leaders would just suck the energy right out of us. They were accomplished psychic vampires, whether they realized it or not. Someone, somewhere, is getting an awful lot of energy out of these thousands of lodge meetings. Ultimately, of course, it is Lucifer, who is delighted to receive it as worship!

This is energy not being expended in godly church activities. These men could be teaching Bible studies, running youth groups, visiting the sick, or doing neighborhood witnessing. But, no, they are sitting in a lodge room watching ancient and dusty mummery being performed while the light of the Holy Spirit within them flickers out.

Over and over, we see vital Christians who join the lodge, don't see the trap, and then gradually it sucks all the life out of their walk with Jesus. It banks their fires of zeal and turns them, ultimately, into dead backsliders. Some stop going to church. Now, this may not happen to all Christian Masons, but if it hasn't, it is only because of God's mercy. The Holy Spirit will not continue to bless a man who continually sups at the devil's table (1 Cor. 10:21, Gen. 6:3). Sooner or later, something will give. Sadly, it is often the church activity.

The Image of Jealousy

The Masonic temple is a temple of witchcraft! There can be little doubt about that. Veiled within its symbols are the deities and even the working tools of witchcraft! As has been shown, the square and compasses are representations of the generative organs—the "sacred altar" of witchcraft! The blazing star at the center of the lodge is the witch's pentagram, symbol of the god of Satanism, Set! The letter *G* stands for generativity, sexual potency.

The resemblances between Freemasonry and witchcraft are manifold and striking and should chill the bones of any Mason. If Freemasonry is so godly, how could it possibly be interchanged by both witches and Satanists so freely?

Beyond that, the point needs to be made that virtually all of the above-mentioned resemblances are part of the ancient practices of pagan antiquity as well. Witches two thousand years ago were doing the same things that Masons are doing today. Masonic writers boast of this (although they don't use the word *witch*, they talk about "mystery religions," but it is the same thing).

Let's face it, the Masonic tie tacks and rings that so many Masons wear proudly to their churches on Sunday are sexual idols. The true God of the Bible is not a sex organ! That may seem a ridiculously obvious statement to make, but the Mason needs to be reminded of it. This is the very "image of jealousy, which provoketh to jealousy" (Ezek. 8:3).

The gods of all the pagan nations around Israel like Baal were all sexual idols! This is precisely what God does not want in His church, and yet all these Masons are flaunting both their idols and their membership.

It is a testimony to the graciousness and loving-kindness of Father God that these churches are not flattened by the breath of His nostrils—that they are not "vomited out" of His mouth (Rev. 3:16). However, both they and their individual members may well be paying a horrible price for their continued winking at the sin of Freemasonry in their camp!

Endnotes

1. Raymond Buckland, *Popular Candle-Burning* (St. Paul, MN: Llewellyn Publications, 1972).

2. For a complete examination of this religion from a Christian perspective, see William J. Schnoebelen, *Wicca: Satan's Little White Lie* (Chino, CA: Chick Publications, 1990).

3. Contrary to popular belief, most male witches do not wish to be called warlocks. The term actually is a derivation of an old English word, meaning "traitor." Today, the word *warlock* is mostly used by male Satanist witches in application to themselves. Few Wiccans would wish to use the term.

4. In witchcraft, the "temple" is frequently not a building, but rather a sacred "Magic Circle" laid down on the floor of a room with great ceremony. It is the sacred space of the Wicca and serves the same function as a temple does to the Mason.

5. Taken from a private copy of the *Book of Shadows* in the author's possession. Copies of this oath, however, can be found in Stewart Farrar's *What Witches Do, the Grimoire of Lady Sheba* (St. Paul, MN: Llewellyn Publications), and June Johns' *King of the Witches*, as well as other writings.

6. Schnoebelen, *Masonry: Beyond the Light* (Chino, CA: Chick Publications, 1991), 146, 155–60, 214–15.

7. See Albert Pike, *Morals and Dogma* (Richmond: L. H. Jenkins, Inc., 1924), 839, 22, 744–45; Manly P. Hall, *The Lost Keys of Freemasonry* (Richmond, VA: Macoy Publishing, 1923), 48.

8. Malcolm Duncan, *Duncan's Ritual Monitor* (New York: David McKay Co., Inc.), 129 and *Tennessee Craftsmen or Masonic Textbook* (Nashville, TN: Grand Lodge of Tennessee, 1983), 17.

9. R. S. Clymer, *The Mysticism of Masonry* (Quakertown, Pennsylvania: The Philosophical Publishing Co., 1900), 47; J.D. Buck, *Symbolism or Mystic Masonry* (Chicago, IL: Regan Publishing Corporation, 1925), 57.

10. Pike, *Morals and Dogma*, 539 and Henry C. Clausen, *Practice and Procedure for the Scottish Rite* (Washington, DC: Supreme Council of the 33° of the Ancient and Accepted Scottish Rite of Freemasonry, 1981), 75–7.

11. Schnoebelen, *Masonry*, 161–78.

12. Ibid., 179–90.

13. The author and his wife were members of a co-Masonic lodge. These are more openly occult and are under the rite of *L'Droit Humaine* (Human Rights Lodge). They admit men and women as equals. Co-Masonry is affiliated with the Theosophical Society and today finds its headquarters in Larkspur, CO.

14. William Schnoebelen and James R. Spencer, *Whited Sepulchers* (Boise, ID: Triple J Publications, 1990), 20.

15. Ibid., 44–50, citing material found in master Satanist Anton LaVey's newsletter, *The Cloven Hoof*, vol. VIII, no. 6.

Eight

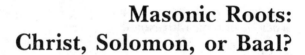

Masonic Roots:
Christ, Solomon, or Baal?

Keith Harris

You have read in other chapters that Freemasonry is a nonsectarian order embracing principles of all religions. Such boasts of universality are a most predominant portion of Masonic belief. Even with varied religious principles, the order must have a beginning or "roots" from which it draws. This chapter is devoted to the roots of Freemasonry, not those of flesh and blood lineage, but the source from which its philosophy is drawn, in particular, the third degree ritual and its true reverence.

As to the origin of the craft, Masons themselves disagree. This lack of unity may stem from personal resentment of evidence or a variety of other reasons. Thus, only those sources deemed reliable must again be our reference. Found in the *Encyclopedia of Freemasonry* under the heading "Christianization of Freemasonry" are the first traces of Masonic reverence: "The principles of Freemasonry preceded the advent of Christianity. Its symbols and its legends are derived from the Solomonic temple and from the people anterior to that. Its religion comes from the ancient priesthood; its faith was that primitive one of Noah and his immediate descendants."[1] We see then that the symbols and legends derive from the Solomonic temple. This aspect refers us to the Legend of the Third Degree ritual, which revolves around King Solomon and Hiram, the widow's son.

We see also that these symbols and legends derive from peoples prior to the Solomonic period. This gives reference to Egypt and their god Osiris, of which Masonic authorities state and one to which we shall later refer. Freemasonry's faith or beliefs are said to have come from Noah and his immediate descendants. We shall examine all the aforementioned aspects in chronological order beginning with Noah.

Roots

After the flood spoken of in Genesis, we find that only eight persons survived that great and awful event. Eight alone to replenish the human race, Noah and his wife, their three sons and their wives. From these came the nations of men: "These are the families of the sons of Noah, after their generations, in their nations: and by these were the nations divided in the earth after the flood" (Gen. 10:32). It is evident that all philosophical beliefs and principles also sprang from, or through, these persons. In Genesis chapter 10, we find listed the descendants, Noah's three sons, Japheth, Ham, and Shem.

In Genesis 11:10–27, we have record of lineage from Shem to Abram (Abraham). Matthew chapter one and Luke chapter three of the New Testament complete the lineage through Abraham to Christ Jesus, revealing the Shemites or Semitic lineage (that of flesh and blood) as that one designated by God as His "chosen people" through which Jesus would later come. Hence, the roots and instructional reference of the Christian faith.

As Christianity permeates every culture and race, flesh and blood lineage is impertinent because Christ accepts whosoever believes to become a partaker of His righteousness. By this spiritual embodiment—known as the Church (born-again believers)—we become of the spiritual house of Abraham (Gal. 3:26–9). It would be interesting were Freemasonry to have its philosophical roots through the principles of the Shemite lineage. However, when compared to Christianity, their origin is different and their histories are dissimilar.

The only substantial evidence given of Noah in Masonry appears in the term *Noahchida* derived from the "legend of the Craft," which reflects that Noah was "the father and founder of the Masonic system of theology." Masonic reference to Noah, however, is heavily fantasized and purely symbolic in nature, as the following demonstrates:

> Such are the Noachic traditions of Masonry, which, though if considered as materials of history, would be worth but little, yet have furnished valuable sources of symbolism, and in that way are full of wise instruction. . . .
>
> After the death of Noah, his sons removed from the region of Mount Ararat, where, until then, they had resided, and "traveling from the East, found a plain in the land of Shinar, and dwelt there." Here they commenced the building of a lofty tower. (Mackey, *Encyclopedia of Freemasonry* [USA: The Masonic History Co., 1921], 514–516)

In the biblical account, Shinar is the name of the land in which were located the cities of Babylon, Erech, Accad, and the root *balal* ("to confound"—Hebrew) and has reference to the confusion of languages at this lofty tower mentioned above (Gen. 11:9).

Significance?

Masonic writings give little insight to the Shemites or Japhethites, but dwell heavily on a descendant of Ham as one of the founders of Masonry—Nimrod. In the *Encyclopedia of Freemasonry* under the heading "Nimrod," we find: "The legend of the Craft in the Old Constitutions refers to Nimrod as one of the founders of Masonry. Thus in the York MS., No. 1, we read: 'At ye makeing of ye Toure of Babell there was Masonrie first much esteemed of, and the King of Babilon yt was called Nimrod was A mason himselfe and loved well Masons.'" Nimrod, a very enterprising man was the most outstanding leader in the period between the flood and Abraham. His widespread popularity is noted in the cities named in connection to him, Birs Nimrud, Tell Nimrud near Bagdad, and the Mound of Nimrud (ancient Calah). Being a "mighty hunter" not only revealed his military might, but also his protectiveness in a time when wild animals were a continual menace. He was also the first to build fenced or fortified cities.[2]

Not only did Nimrod "love well Masons," they too esteem him of great personage for his work in Masonry. Many Masons who profess Christianity refer to Genesis 10:9 to substantiate his greatness and virtue in the phrase "mighty hunter before the Lord." However, a minute study of this thought and phrase will reveal his virtue to be quite the opposite than what is commonly accepted.

The word *mighty* (*gibbowr*—Hebrew) means warrior, tyrant. A tyrant is one who exercises power in a harsh, cruel manner. Nimrod is also known in history as a hunter of men. The latter part of the phrase "before the Lord" stems around the word *before* which comes from the Hebrew word *paniym* meaning "the face (as the part that turns)." This reveals to us that Nimrod was a tyrant who turned his face from the Lord. This is why the Hebrew people referred to him as "the rebel" or "rebellious one."

Many cities and nations had for their chief god their founder; such was the case with Nimrod. To make this "god" more real and honorable, images were made to represent him; later, the images themselves came to be worshipped. This was also true of certain constellations being attributed to him after his death. Thus, the chief god of Babylon, and Ninevah, Nimrod, had images referring to him. These images glorified his attributes as protector, leader, god of war, knowledge, etc.

It was during the building of the tower of Babel, also attributed to Nimrod, that God confused the languages

of the people, and the building was stopped. The Bible
states that the whole world was of one speech (language)
prior to this event (Gen. 11). At the "confusion of languages" people could no longer speak the name of their
god. Thus, Nimrod, their chief god, was now known by
multiple names due to multiple languages.

As Nimrod had so many things attributed to him, it
was only reasonable for peoples, now in segregation, to
adopt the portion of belief best interpreted by each group.
Thus, there were diverse religious attributes and beliefs,
but peoples still remaining reverent to their god. We find
such names for this revered god (Nimrod) in Scripture as
Chemosh, Molock, Merodach, Remphan, Tamuz, and Baal,
to mention only a few of the some thirty-eight biblical
titles plus numerous representatives of these "gods." Under the heading of "Nimrod" found in *Halley's Bible Handbook*, we discover that "Babylonia was long known as the
"Land of Nimrod." He was afterward deified, his name
being identical with 'Merodach.'"[3]

And, under the heading of "Merodach" in *Tyndales
New Bible Dictionary*, we find that "Merodach is the Heb.
form of the Babylonian divine name Marduk. . . . Marduk
was the primary deity of Babylon and was later called by
his epithet Bel (Ba'al), so that his defeat was synonymous
with that of his people (Jer. 50:2) as was that of the earlier
Canaanite Ba'al."[4] Baal worship was a form of the old sun
worship, for Baal (Nimrod as we have seen) was represented by the sun. Many names throughout biblical and
classical history appear and refer to Nimrod. These formed
what is referred to as the ancient mysteries.

Egypt

Albert Pike, in his book *Morals and Dogma* refers to
the ancient mysteries and Freemasonry as being identical,
with exceptions found only in that of progressive alter-
ations.[5] As all ancient mysteries independently examined
would be a timely and spacious task, it is only necessary
to expound on the mystery religion that Masonry itself
deems true: "Egypt has always been considered as the

birthplace of the mysteries. It was there that the ceremonies of initiation were first established. It was there that
truth was first veiled in allegory, and the dogmas of religion were first imparted under symbolic forms."[6]

We have found that Masonic symbols and legends
derive from peoples anterior to the Solomonic temple.
Egypt is a major source of such. "To Egypt, therefore,
Masons have always looked with peculiar interest as the
cradle of that mysterious science of symbolism whose
peculiar modes of teaching they alone, of all modern
institutions, have preserved to the present day."[7]

We have found also that the Masonic "religion" comes
from the ancient priesthood. One might think this refers
to the Levitical priesthood of the Bible, however, the
priesthood of Egypt is their reference: "The priesthood
of Egypt constituted a sacred caste, in whom the sacredotal
functions were hereditary."[8]

The Connection

Although varied countries had many gods, only certain gods (or exalted positions) were represented by the
sun and moon. Albert Pike, in *Morals and Dogma*, writes,
"We know that the Egyptians worshipped the Sun, under
the name of Osiris."[9]

Pike also connects Baal worship and Osiris as identical:

> The Goths had three festivals; the most magnifi-
> cent of which commenced at the winter solstice,
> and was celebrated in honor of Thor, the Prince
> of the Power of the Air. . . .
>
> Thor was the Sun, the Egyptian Osiris and Kneph,
> the Phoenician Bel or Baal. The initiations were
> had in huge intricate caverns, terminating, as all
> the Mithriac caverns did, in a spacious vault, where
> the candidate was *brought to light*. [emphasis added]
> (Albert Pike, *Morals and Dogma*, 368)

The legend of Osiris, the Egyptian god, is significant
to Masonry due to the ritual of the Third Degree as well

as other teachings which are deep-rooted in Egyptian legend. This legend and the legend of Hiram Abiff, a ritual familiar to all Third Degree Masons, have similarities which cannot be overlooked when compared.

Osiris Legend

Osiris was the chief god of Egypt, the son and husband of Isis. Osiris is said to have been killed by his jealous brother Typhon by trickery. Osiris was nailed in a chest and cast into the Nile. Later, his dead body was cast up at Byblos in Phoenicia and left at the foot of a Tamarind tree. Isis retrieved his body only to lose it again to the jealous brother who then cut him into fourteen pieces, which he scattered around the kingdom. Isis again went in search of Osiris and found all the body parts except the phallus, which had been eaten by a crab in the Nile. Isis then made a phallus, which was to be sacred (origin of the Obelisk).

She embalmed him thus claiming restoration and gave rise to the concept that the immortality of the soul was dependent on the preservation of the body. Osiris was afterward known as the Lord of the Underworld. He was also god of the sun and god of fertility, worshipped in orgiastic sex rituals.

Third Degree Masonic Ritual

As Masonry has preserved the Egyptian science of symbolism, it is apparent that an observation or ritual exists projecting from Egypt—the ritual of the Third Degree or Master Mason Degree. This ritual is centered around the supposition of King Solomon and Hiram.

As the story goes, Hiram of Tyre, and a widow's son, was working on Solomon's Temple when approached by three ruffians desiring the Master's word. The time was high twelve, and all other workers were out for refreshment. When Hiram refused on three occasions, or confrontations, to give the word, he was killed after a blow to the forehead with a setting maul by the third ruffian. Hiram was then buried in the temple until low twelve, or midnight, at which time the ruffians return to take his body (westerly) to again bury him. King Solomon, the following day, found him missing and the craft in confusion and desired to know the cause.

The workmen had already searched for Hiram but without success. Thus, King Solomon again sent out a search. After several days of searching, and upon return, the party stopped to rest and refresh themselves. By accident they discovered the newly made grave of Hiram beneath an acacia tree. At this time they hear lamenting at a nearby cleft, the self-impending penalties (same as oath penalties) of Jubela, Jubelo, and Jubelum, the ruffians. Thus, the search was over and the murderers caught.

The candidate for Third Degree initiation, after preliminary ritual, is found lying on the floor representing the death of Hiram. The Junior Warden takes hold of the candidate's right hand and attempts to "raise" him from death but without success. His hand slips from the candidates hand symbolizing the slipping off of the skin and an insufficient grip. The Senior Warden then makes an attempt but fails, due symbolically to the flesh cleaving from the bone—again, an insufficient grip.

The Worshipful Master, symbolizing King Solomon, successfully raises the candidate using the "Strong Grip" or "Lion's Paw Grip." The candidate is thus raised on the five points of fellowship—foot to foot, knee to knee, breast to breast, hand to back, cheek to cheek. In this position, the Master gives the Grand Masonic Word: Mah-Hah-Bone. This raising of the candidate is to symbolize the resurrection, which is the object of the degree (The Hebrew rendition of Mah-Hah-Bone is "What! the builder?").

This ritual, has of course, a Masonic/Christian interpretation, which according to Albert Pike goes as follows: "The murder of Hiram, his burial, and his being raised again by the Master, are symbols, both of the Redeemer; and of the death and burial in sins of the natural man, and his being raised again to a new life, or born again, by the direct action of the Redeemer."[10]

We must note that the above ritual is only symbolic as is stated here, that is, not the actual thing. We must remember also that the Blue Degrees (first three) are intentionally misled by false interpretation. Thus, this ritual does not actually refer to Hiram, especially when compared to the biblical account.

Masonry claims that Hiram died "during the work," yet the Bible tells us that Hiram (Huram) "finished the work" and mentions nothing of his death and miraculous recovery at the hand of Solomon. We also find that this was God's house, not Solomon's: "And Huram finished the work that he was to make for king Solomon for the house of God" (2 Chron. 4:11). And, as the legends of Osiris and Hiram are compared, we see both died at the hand of a brother; they were twice searched for; both were found at the foot of a tree; and, both had a loss: Osiris has a missing body part; the Master's word is lost.

The following information tells us that the third degree ritual is not actually that of Hiram nor Christ, but the epic of Osiris. Thus, in the Third Degree of Masonry, the initiate is actually entering into the death, burial, and resurrection of Osiris. Speaking of the degree of "Knight of the Brazen Serpent," Pike elaborates for us:

> While it teaches the necessity of reformation as well as repentance, as a means of obtaining mercy and forgiveness, it is also devoted to an explanation of the symbols of Masonry; and especially to those which are connected with that ancient and universal legend, of which that of Khir-Om Abi is but a variation; that legend which, representing a murder or a death, and a restoration to life, by a drama which figure Osiris, Isis and Horus, . . . and many another representative of active and passive powers of Nature, taught the Initiates in the Mysteries that the rule of Evil and Darkness is but temporary, and that of Light and Good will be eternal. [Khir-Om Abi is Hiram Abiff] (Albert Pike, *Morals and Dogma*, 435)

The "raised" candidate is stated as being raised into a philosophy of regeneration, or the new birth of all things. In effect, he is becoming born again through the power of Masonry.

This reverence, as that of Egypt, reveals the worship or exaltation of the things of nature. Albert Pike says this of nature and Osiris: "Everything good in Nature comes from Osiris."[11] This typifies not only life out of death, but the regeneration of the things of nature or "generative power" (sexual reproductive power). In addition, Pike writes that "Osiris and Isis were the sun and Moon, is attested by many ancient writers"[12] which, as we have seen is reference to Baal or Nimrod, one of the founders of Masonry. Thus, Osiris, Nimrod, Baal, Merodach, etc., are synonymous, that is, one and the same.

This Masonic reverence for the sun is familiar to all Masons, even if unknowingly, in the symbol of the All-Seeing Eye: "The Sun was termed by the Greeks the Eye of Jupiter, and the Eye of the World; and his is the All-Seeing Eye in our Lodges ['his' refers to Osiris]."[13] And, speaking of those of Thebes, an ancient city in Upper Egypt, Pike further mentions that "soon they personified the sun, and worshipped him under the name of Osiris, and transmuted the legend of his descent among the Winter Signs, into a fable of his death, his descent into the infernal regions, and his resurrection.[14]

It is noteworthy to mention that the officers at the opening of lodge ceremonies—Worshipful Master, Senior, and Junior Wardens—are seated in stations in the East, South, and West. In religious symbolism of Freemasonry, they represent the sun at "his" rising, "his" meridian, and "his" setting.

Many Masons today are duped into the same worship of Baal as of old. The All-Seeing Eye, they are told, represents God, as does the letter *G*. The name God, however, is mistaken in quite the same way as the name Baal in the Old Testament. The name Baal carried the meaning "lore, possessor," which, by name, was very easily mistaken for the God of Abraham who is also called Lord. The manner in which each was worshipped, however, was quite different and obvious when compared. Such is the Masonic/Christian conflict!

With all the different names for Nimrod, yet many similarities in cultural attributes, philosophers, in later years, began to congregate those things common in belief to again philosophically regain the once admired religion (possibly without being aware of such). It was only natural for elite philosophers to recognize the most elaborate and dogmatic of these peoples from which to draw their assumptions. Egypt was that main source, especially for Freemasonry, for Freemasonry is a mystical, speculative search: "The history of Masonry is the history of Philosophy."[15]

The roots of Freemasonry lie in Egyptian legend with reverence to Osiris or Baal (Nimrod), thus becoming Baal worship. Not Baal worship fictitiously stated, but actual Baal worship through ritual and appellation.

Its faith is indeed that primitive one of Noah and his immediate descendants, particularly Nimrod, who was deified under the name Merodach, Baal, Osiris, etc. The Solomonic legend was conjured in order for Christians to appear adaptable, for Solomon never raised anyone from death to life. The only possibility of this was through symbolism when Solomon did "evil in the sight of the Lord": "Then did Solomon build an high place for Chemosh the abomination of Moab, in the hill that is before Jerusalem, and for Molech, the abomination of the children of Ammon. And likewise did he for all his strange wives, which burnt incense and sacrificed unto their gods" (1 Kings 11:7–8).

The tribes of Israel were often seduced into the worship of Nimrod (Baal, Osiris), not only because of the confusing name *Baal*, but due largely to their Egyptian bondage. As a nation, Israel is said to have had its birth at the Exodus from Egypt. During the Egyptian bondage, they multiplied in number under the influence of Egyptian custom and worship.

After the Exodus from Egypt, the gaiety and licentious character of the Egyptian god was soon revealed at the absence of their leader Moses. Moses had gone up Mt. Sinai where he received the Ten Commandments from the Lord. Upon his return, he found the Israelites worshipping an Egyptian image, a symbol of Osiris and generative power, a golden calf. In *Smith's Bible Dictionary*, the calf is described as an "image for worship made at Sinai in imitation of the Apis of Egypt, from the jewelry borrowed of the Egyptians (Ex. xxxii. 2). Not of solid gold, but of wood, gilded and plated with gold [as the emblem of Osiris-Apis was made]."[16]

The Israelites were to worship the God of Abraham, Isaac, and Jacob, not the "gods" of surrounding peoples. They were warned of such: "Thou shalt not bow down to their gods, nor serve them, nor do after their works: but thou shalt utterly overthrow them, and quite break down their images" (Exod. 12:12). Moses undoubtedly recognized the symbol—for he was reared by Pharaoh's daughter and "was learned in all the wisdom of the Egyptians" (Acts 7:22). In an outburst of anger, Moses broke the tables of stone containing the Ten Commandments. This Israelite idolatry brought about the death of around three thousand people. In addition, "the Lord plagued the people, because they made the calf, which Aaron made" (Exod. 32:35).

The calf was always a bull, with horns, representing sexual strength, or generative power. Paganism is always sexual in its outworkings and, ultimately, phallus worship. Time and again, Israel was seduced into such worship (Deut. 13:6, 7). Many representatives, in one fashion or another, were those of the false god Baal (Nimrod, Osiris). Canaanite gods, Assyrian gods, the gods of the Ammorites and Moabites, to mention only a few strange gods, were worshipped.

In *Unger's Bible Dictionary*, speaking of idolatry among the Ten Tribes of Israel, we find: "Jeroboam, fresh from his recollections of the Apis worship of Egypt, erected golden calves at Beth-el and Dan, and by this crafty state policy severed effectively the kingdoms of Judah and Israel (1 Kings 12:26-33)."[17] ("Apis," the Bull, was also a symbol of the strength of Nimrod.)

Christian Concern

With all the fallacies throughout our land and country, there is none that can effectively topple Christianity. Only when such outside influence is allowed to filter into Christian congregations through church membership, commissions, and leadership positions, is the Church world affected. Freemasonry is not an outside influence. It is an inside influence!

As Jeroboam effectively severed Judah and Israel, Freemasonry is slowly severing Christian witness. The Holy Spirit has vacated so many of our congregations and for just cause. Baal worship is still at large! Satan is once again using the oldest strategy in the world—conquer the enemy from within to best conquer him from without. Joshua says:

> Now therefore fear the Lord, and serve him in sincerity and in truth: and put away the gods which your fathers served on the other side of the flood, and in Egypt; and serve ye the Lord. And if it seem evil unto you to serve the Lord, choose you this day whom ye will serve; whether the gods which your fathers served that were on the other side of the flood, or the gods of the Amorites, in whose land ye dwell: but as for me and my house, we will serve the Lord. (Josh. 24:14–5)

But, there is an escape, an out for the Christian willing to take a godly stand against the darkness. I pray each reader will take that godly stand today! "But all things that are reproved are made manifest by the light: for whatsoever doth make manifest is light" (Eph. 5:13).

Endnotes

1. Albert G. Mackey, *Encyclopedia of Freemasonry* (The Masonic History Company, 1921), 148-149.

2. Dr. Henry H. Halley, *Halley's Bible Handbook* (Grand Rapids, MI: Zondervan Publishing House, 1965), 82–84.

3. Ibid., 82.

4. *Tyndales New Bible Dictionary* (Wheaton, IL: Tyndale House Publishers, Inc.), 761–762.

5. Albert Pike, *Morals and Dogma* (Richmond: L. H. Jenkins, Inc., 1924), 624.

6. Mackey, *Encyclopedia of Freemasonry*, 232.

7. Ibid., 232.

8. Ibid., 232.

9. Pike, *Morals and Dogma*, 406.

10. Ibid., 640.

11. Ibid., 476.

12. Ibid., 476, 477.

13. Ibid., 477.

14. Ibid., 477.

15. Ibid., 540.

16. Smith, *Smith's Bible Dictionary* (Baton Rouge, LA: Jimmy Swaggart Ministries), 45.

17. M. F. Unger, *Unger's Bible Dictionary* (Chicago, IL: Moody Press, 1966), 605.

Nine

Freemasonry and the Twentieth Century Occult Revival

David Carrico

Freemasonry is an occult secret society, and all Freemasons have aligned themselves with the occult. This is the obvious conclusion that people with just a casual knowledge of the lodge are forced to realize. The word *occult* means deliberately kept hidden, not revealed to others.[1] How can Freemasonry avoid being classified as occult when the Mason is forbidden by oath not to reveal what goes on behind the closed doors of the lodge even to his wife or his fellow church members. All Freemasons have definitely participated in occult activities. This is an opinion that the Masonic book *The Royal Arch: Its Hidden Meaning* heartily agrees with.

Many Freemasons shudder at the word *occult*, which comes from the Latin, meaning to cover, to conceal from public scrutiny, and the profane. But, anyone studying Freemasonry cannot avoid classifying Freemasonry among occult teachings.[2]

We will be studying some of the powerful people and organizations that have played a part in the modern occult revival, and we will find as we study their teachings that they all have one common denominator: Freemasonry.

Freemasonry: The Devil's Playground

Anton LaVey, the high priest of the Church of Satan states that "Masonic orders have contained the most influential men in many governments, and virtually every occult order has many Masonic roots."[3] Freemasonry is not just an occult secret society. Freemasonry has served for over two hundred years as a fertile recruiting ground for other occult orders. Men who have come together to practice Masonry have many times down through the years formed other organizations to plunge even deeper into the occult.

The Illuminati

According to our research, the first group that used the Masonic lodge for their evil designs was the infamous Bavarian Illuminati. This secret society was officially formed by Adam Weishaupt, professor of Canon Law at Ingolstadt University, on 1 May 1776. As the evil plans of the Illuminati began to leak out, brave men took a stand and raised their voices in protest.

One such man was John Robinson, a professor of Natural Philosophy at Edinburgh University and general secretary of the Royal Society of Edinburgh. In his book *Proofs of a Conspiracy*, which was originally published in 1798, Robinson documented how Masonry served as the nursery school for the Illuminati. It was then discovered that this group and several associated lodges were the preparation school for another order of Masons, who called themselves The Illuminated, and that the express aim of this order was to abolish Christianity and overturn all civil government.[4]

Helena Petrovna Blavatsky

The leaders of the New Age movement have also found a friend in the friendly confines of the Masonic lodges. In the last two centuries, Freemasonry and the New Age movement have been intricately entwined. The

Scottish Rite Journal of the Southern Jurisdiction was previously called the *New Age Magazine* between 1903 and 1990. Freemason Lynn F. Perkins wrote a book in 1972, titled *New Age Youth and Masonry: What Every High School and College Graduate Should Know About Masonry.*

This book was dedicated to those of oncoming generations of youth who would build and operate the new order of the ages.[5] He also wrote another book called *Masonry in The New Age*. Both of these books are listed for sale in the 1991 Macoy Publishing and Masonic Supply Co. catalog. The woman heralded as the "Mother" of the modern New Age movement is Helena Petrovna Blavatsky (1831–1891). Blavatsky was born in Russia and was known for her violent temper and her ability to swear in several languages. This behavior was no doubt intensified as a result of her drug addiction to hashish. She traveled all over the world lecturing and practicing the occult, but her greatest impact, by far, was through her writings.

Her most famous book, *The Secret Doctrine*, is one of the foundational occult works of all time. Her preeminently wicked book made no distinction between the serpent and the God of the Bible and taught that Satan was the one that made man into a god: "Once that the key to Genesis is in our hands, the scientific and symbolical Kabalah unveils the secret. The Great Serpent of the garden of Eden and the Lord God are identical."[6] She continues, saying, "Thus Satan, once he ceases to be viewed in the superstitious, dogmatic, unphilosophical spirit of the Churches, grows into the grandiose image of one who makes of a terrestrial, a divine Man."[7]

The Theosophical Society

Blavatsky's *The Secret Doctrine* and the organization she helped to found, the Theosophical Society, has certainly had an impact on our culture. *The Secret Doctrine* was the first book that Sirhan Sirhan requested after he was jailed for the murder of Robert Kennedy. Adolf Hitler kept a copy of *The Secret Doctrine* at his bedside and was profoundly influenced by it.

Adolf Hitler was a disciple of Madame Blavatsky and was initiated into the meaning of her secret doctrines. He was tutored by men who were formerly theosophists themselves and had theosophists at his side until the very end of the war.[8] This favorite book of Adolf Hitler's was also a favorite of Freemasonry's greatest philosopher, Thirty-third Degree Mason Manly P. Hall. Hall spoke with unrestrained praise for Blavatsky's writings:

> *The Secret Doctrine* and *Isis Unveiled* are Madame Blavatsky's gifts to humanity, and to those whose vision can pierce the menacing clouds of imminent disaster it is no exaggeration to affirm that these writings are the most vital literary contribution to the modern world. No more can they be compared with other books than can the light of the sun be compared with the lamp of the glow-worm. *The Secret Doctrine* assumes the dignity of a scripture. (Manly P. Hall, *The Phoenix: An Illustrated Review of Occultism and Philosophy* [Los Angeles, CA: The Philosophical Research Society, 1960], 122)

Blavatsky's organization, the Theosophical Society, was founded in 1875. Freemason Henry Steel Olcott was the president, with Freemason George H. Felt as vice president and high-ranking American Mason Charles Sothern as a member. Also, among the early members was the most powerful American Mason of all time, Albert Pike, Grand Commander of the Scottish Rite. Madame Blavatsky was such a favorite of Freemasons that she was issued a Masonic certificate in the Ancient and Primitive Rite of Masonry in 1877.

Annie Besant and the Theosophical Society

In 1907, Annie Besant became the head of the Theosophical Society. Besant continued Blavatsky's love for Masonry by becoming a leader and earning the Thirty-third Degree in Co-Masonry, an order with rites that admitted women as well as men. On 19 February 1922, an alliance between Mrs. Besant's Co-Masonry and the Grand

Orient of France was celebrated at the Grand Temple of the Droite Humain in Paris.[9]

C. W. Leadbeater and the Theosophical Society

During the time Annie Besant was head of the Theosophical Society, she labored to promote a young man from India, Jiddu Krishnamurti, as the Messiah. Her right-hand man in this endeavor was Thirty-third Degree Mason, C.W. Leadbeater. This Freemason had a passionate desire for the deeper workings of the occult. Some sources claim Leadbeater was a pedophile homosexual.[10]

When the dark side of Freemasonry begins to be revealed and discussed, the question invariably arises: Does participation in Masonic rituals lead to demon invasion and control? C.W. Leadbeater answers that question for us most decisively from an insiders point of view. Leadbeater does more than give an affirmative answer to our question. He proceeds to describe the demon spirits he received in the various degrees of Freemasonry:

> The 30th degree brings its Angel also, of appropriate character—a great blue Deva of the First Ray, who lends his strength to the Knight K.H., somewhat as the crimson Angel assists the Ex. and perf. Bro. of the Rose-Croix. The 33rd degree gives two such splendid fellow-workers—spirits of gigantic size as compared to humanity, and radiantly white in colour. (C.W. Leadbeater, *The Hidden Life in Freemasonry* [Adyar, Madras, India: The Theosophical Publishing House, 1928], 336)

> The 33rd degree links the Sovereign Grand Inspector General with the Spiritual King of the World Himself, That Mightiest of Adepts who stands at the head of the Great White Lodge, in whose strong hands lie the destinies of earth. . . . (326)

> Yet when one of these bright Spirits is attached to us by a Masonic ceremony we must not think of him either as a director or as an attendant, but simply as a co-worker and a brother. (334)

Alice A. and Foster Bailey

Alice A. Bailey was the reigning queen of the New Age movement until her death in the 1970s. She wrote over twenty books with the help of her spirit guide, the Tibetan master Dwjhal Khul. Mrs. Bailey spoke plainly and truthfully about the fact that the Masonic lodge was the training school for the leaders of the occult world. She said of Freemasonry: "It is a far more occult organization than can be realized, and is intended to be the training school for the coming advanced occultists."[11]

Together with her husband, Thirty-second Degree Mason Foster Bailey, Alice Bailey labored to bring in the reign of the New Age Christ. Foster states that "the most important re-orientation in the Hierarchy is the united focus on preparation for the reappearance of the Christ among men."[12] And, "the Christ is a living man today. He is a great world executive and is actively working to help humanity to grow up spiritually, but not seeking or wanting to control us."[13] Furthermore, Foster points out that "the Christ and the hierarchy are focused on new age actions and when externalized will use new age techniques."[14]

Foster Bailey also ridiculed the Christ of the Bible and heralded the false gospel of the New Age Christ: "The Christian doctrine that he comes as a Christian to save us from hell and for some distant judgment date is a hangover from humanity's childhood days. He does not come to save us but to help us save ourselves."[15]

Foster Bailey wrote articles for Masonic magazines and lectured at Masonic lodge halls. His book, *The Spirit of Masonry*, is still sold in the Macoy Publishing and Masonic Supply Co. catalog. It is sobering to read in his book how this powerful New Age leader spoke of Masonry as the universal religion.

> Is it not possible from a contemplation of this side of Masonic teaching that it may provide all that is necessary for the formulation of a universal religion? May it not be true, as has been said, that if

all religions and Scriptures were blotted out and only Masonry were left in the world we could still recover the great plan of salvation? Most earnestly should all true Masons consider this point. . . .

A revitalized Masonry, made up of Masons true to their obligations and realizing the Mystic Tie that binds them all together in one true brotherhood, would also provide a platform so universal that it would meet the need of thinkers of all kinds and of every school of thought. It would thus not only meet a religious need by providing a universal religion, but would also satisfy the mental need felt by all broad-minded thinkers at this time. (Foster Bailey, *The Spirit of Masonry* [London: Lucis Press Limited, 1957], 109)

Aleister Crowley: Father of Modern Satanism

The most disturbing example of someone being recruited out of Freemasonry into more bizarre occult orders is that of Thirty-third Degree Mason Aleister Crowley. During his lifetime, Crowley was proclaimed by the press as the most wicked man alive. Crowley's perverted life left a string of casualties among those who were foolish enough to get close to this evil man. Crowley's first wife, Rose, entered an insane asylum in 1911; his second wife, Maria, entered an asylum in 1931, two years after her marriage to Crowley. In a locked room with only Crowley and his son present, Crowley performed a ritual in which his son died. On a London street in 1934, a nineteen-year-old girl rushed up to him and declared that she wanted to have his baby. Crowley took her to bed. She, too, later entered an asylum.[16]

Just a brief autobiographic sketch of Crowley's life is like an evening swim in a sewer. Crowley called himself the "Beast 666" and Leila Waddell, his mistress, displayed the mark of the beast that was tattooed between her breasts. If there ever was a man that was more wicked than Crowley, it would be hard to imagine. Crowley was a homosexual and a drug addict that opposed Christianity with a hatred that was frightening. He said, "To me, every dirty act was simply a sacrament of sin, a passionately religious protest against Christianity, which was for me the symbol of all vileness, meanness, treachery, falsehood and oppression."[17]

O.T.O.: Ordo Templi Orientis and Freemason, Theodor Reuss

One of the most alarming things about Crowley's life was the way that he went from Freemasonry into the cult of the O.T.O. (Ordo Templi Orientis). Crowley tells in his own words how Freemason Theodor Reuss recruited him into the O.T.O.:

> Although I was admitted to the thirty-third and last degree of Freemasonry so long ago as 1900, it was not until the summer of 1912 that my suspicion was confirmed. I speak of my belief that behind the frivolities and convivialities of our greatest institution lay in truth a secret ineffable and miraculous, potent to control the forces of Nature, and not only to make men brethren, but to make them divine. But at the time I speak of a man [Theodor Reuss] came to me, a man of those mysterious masters of esoteric Freemasonry who are alike its Eyes and its Brains, and who exist in its midst unknown, often, even to its acknowledged chiefs. . . . This man had been watching my occult career for some years, and deemed me now worthy to partake in the Greater Mysteries. (Kenneth Grant, *Aleister Crowley and the Hidden God* [New York, NY: Samuel Weiser, 1974], 174)

This certainly shows that members of other occult orders can work within Freemasonry often times without the knowledge of the actual leaders of the lodge. The O.T.O. was founded in 1895 by the Austrian Freemason Karl Kellner. Freemason Theodor Reuss became its leader after Kellner's death. Reuss started a magazine called the *Oriflame* in 1902 with the help of Freemason Franz

Hartman. A 1912 jubilee edition of the magazine revealed information about what the O.T.O. activities really were. "Our order possesses the KEY which opens up all Masonic and Hermetic secrets, namely, the teaching of sexual magic, and this teaching explains, without exception, all the secrets of Nature, all the symbolism of Freemasonry and all systems of religion."[18]

Aleister Crowley and the O.T.O.

In 1912, while holding the rank of Thirty-third Degree Mason, Aleister Crowley became the head of the British O.T.O. The teachings and the practices of the O.T.O. were amazingly disgusting. A very brief description of their degrees is as follows:

> Today's literature about sex magic relies heavily on practices which were already common in the O.T.O. or in its later development by Aleister Crowley. . . . The division is as follows: VIII degree O.T.O. = autoerotic practice IX degree O.T.O. = heteroerotic practice XI degree O.T.O. = homoerotic practice. This is the traditional sex-magic practice as performed under Crowley. (Frater U.D., Secrets of the German Sex Magicians [St. Paul, MN: Llewellyn Publications, 1991], 138)

Also, "Thirty-third degree Aleister Crowley proudly called his cult of the O.T.O. 'true freemasonry.' I claim for my system that it satisfies all possible requirements of true freemasonry. It offers a rational basis for universal brotherhood and for universal religion."[19]

How close is the connection between Freemasonry and the O.T.O.? Masonic historian Francis King reveals a closer connection than most Freemasons would ever dare to admit:

> For the O.T.O. not only had, as we shall see, connections with spurious and clandestine Masonic groups but functioned as a recruiting office for one of these for in the "Classification of Members by Degrees" appended to Ruess's document is

clearly stated that "candidates are made Freemasons by the Directing Members (Fratres Superiores)
of the O.T.O." (Frances King, *The Secret Rituals of
the O.T.O.* [New York, NY: Samuel Weiser, 1973],
13.)

The fact that Crowley was the head of the O.T.O.
while holding the rank of Thirty-third Degree Mason
should forever explode the myth that Freemasonry is a
Christian organization. Crowley spoke openly and can-
didly about his Masonic honors.

This view was confirmed when The Arcane Schools
of John Yarker came to me for review. I wrote to
the author, who recognized my title to the 33rd
degree and conferred on me the grades of 95
degree Memphis and the 90 degree Mizraim. It
seemed as if I had some how turned a tap. From
this time on I lived in a perfect shower of diplo-
mas, from Bucharest to Salt Lake City. I possess
more exalted titles than I have ever been able to
count. I am supposed to know more secret signs,
tokens, passwords, grandwords, grips, and so on,
than I could actually learn in a dozen lives. An
elephant would break down under the insignia I
am entitled to wear. (John Symonds and Kenneth
Grant, *The Confessions of Aleister Crowley* [New York,
NY: Bantam Books, 1971], 684)

In *The Confessions of Aleister Crowley*, Crowley spoke
with great admiration about the Royal Arch degree: "I
supposed myself to have reached the summit of success
when I restored the Secret Word of the Royal Arch. In
this case, tradition had preserved the Word almost in-
tact."[20]

It is perfectly understandable that this hater of Chris-
tianity would love the Royal Arch degree of Freemasonry.
In this degree, Freemasons blaspheme the God of the
Bible by uniting God's name with pagan gods. The secret
word of the Royal Arch that Crowley is referring to is Jah-
Bul-On. The *Jah* represents Jehovah, *Bul* represents the

pagan god Baal, and *On* represents the Egyptian sun god. It is no wonder Crowley's Satanic heart jumped for joy when he was able to blaspheme the God of the Bible by uniting the true God with the pagan god Baal to whom human children were sacrificed. The Scriptures tell us "they have also built the high places of Baal, to burn their sons with fire for burnt offerings to Baal, which I did not command or speak, nor did it come into My mind" (Jer. 19:5).

The meaning of the secret word in the Royal Arch degree is confirmed by an excellent authority, *The Encyclopedia of Freemasonry* by Albert G. Mackey. Baal signifies lord or master and occurs several times in the Bible as a part of the names of various gods. Alone, the word applies to the sun-god, the supreme male deity of the Syro-Phoenician nations. For an account of his worship read First Kings chapter eighteen. With Jah and On, it has been introduced into the Royal Arch system as a representative of the Tetragrammaton.[21]

The O.T.O. describes itself as an organization that is dedicated to follow the doctrine of Crowley. The Ordo Templi Orientis (O.T.O.) is an Initiatic Body composed of men and women who have accepted the principles of *The Book of the Law*, which was transmitted through Aleister Crowley (1875–1947).

> The Book is conceived to be a perfect transmission of the divine, freed from any defects of human interference. As such, it is a luminous vehicle of Truth that can serve as an infallible guide to human conduct. . . . Aleister Crowley will at least be remembered as the greatest occult genius of the twentieth century. . . . His influence on modern occultism is incalculable, penetrating every Western school. (Hymenaeus, ed., "Aleister Crowley: The Master Therion," The Equinox [1990], vol. 3, no. 10:87)

Any cult that follows the teachings of Crowley must be taken very seriously. The following quotes are from

The Book of Law that the O.T.O. endorsed as a perfect transmission of the divine and a luminous vehicle of truth that can serve as an infallible guide to human conduct.

> 11. Worship me with fire & blood; worship me with swords & with spears. Let the woman be girt with a sword before me: let blood flow to my name. Trample down the Heathen; be upon them, o warrior, I will give you Petrovnaou of their flesh to eat 12. Sacrifice cattle, little and big: after a child. . . . 24. The best blood is of the moon, monthly: then the fresh blood of a child, or dropping from the host of heaven: then of enemies; then of priest or of the worshippers: last of some beast, no matter what. . . . 51. With my Hawk's head I peck at the eyes of Jesus as he hangs upon the cross. . . . 60. There is no law beyond Do what thou wilt. (The Equinox, vol. 3, no. 10:39, 40, 42, 43)

The following quotes from Crowley's *Magick in Theory and Practice* will further prove our concern.

> For the highest spiritual working one must accordingly choose that victim which contains the greatest and purest force. A male child of perfect innocence and high intelligence is the most satisfactory and suitable victim. . . . But the bloody sacrifice, though more dangerous, is more efficacious; and for nearly all purposes human sacrifice is the best. . . . In the Sacrifice during Invocation, however, it may be said without fear of contradiction that the death of the victim should coincide with the supreme invocation. (Aleister Crowley, *Magick in Theory and Practice* [New York, NY: Magickal Childe Publishing, Inc. 1990], 95–6)

Rosicrucian Society

As we continue our study of Freemasonry and the occult, we need to look at another secret order that has networked with Freemasonry for many years, the

Rosicrucian Society. Much could be written about the various Rosicrucian orders and their relationship to the lodge, but for the purpose of our study we will be mentioning only one: the Rosicruciana in Anglia. One had to be at least a Master Mason to belong to this organization, and it is of particular interest because the members of this secret order gave birth to yet another secret society, The Golden Dawn.

In some respects, Westcott's *Hermetic Order of the Golden Dawn* was a by-product of his connection with a Masonic "Rosicrucian" fraternity called the Rosicrucian Society of England, also known as the Societas Rosicruciana in Anglia, or more familiarly as the Soc. Ros. Membership was confined to Master Masons. It was not a Masonic lodge but an esoteric society of Freemasons who were interested in occultism, the Cabala in particular, and Masonic symbolism.[22]

All three of the original founders of the Golden Dawn were Freemasons: Dr. William Wynn Westcott, Dr. William Woodman, and S.L. MacGregor Mathers. As we shall see, the ties between the Golden Dawn and the Masonic lodge go much deeper than the fact that all were Freemasons. Dr. William Wynn Westcott's interests were occultism and Freemasonry. In order to practice ritual magic, he established an occult secret society called the Golden Dawn in London in 1888. Since its founding, it has been one of the most secretive and influential of all occult orders.

Madam Blavatsky was so excited about the existence of the Golden Dawn that she made an intriguing announcement calling the order "The Hermetic Students of the G.D. in the Outer" in the June 1889 issue of her Theosophical periodical, *Lucifer*.[23] World renowned witches, Janet and Stewart Farrar, authors of *A Witches Bible Compleat*, give credit to the Freemasons of the Golden Dawn for the modern cult explosion that we are experiencing today. They state:

> It is generally agreed that the biggest single influence in the modern expansion of ritual magic, and

the occult explosion in general, in the Western world, was the Golden Dawn. This magical fraternity, founded by Freemasons at the end of the 19th century, developed a complex ritual system with ten degrees of initiation relating to the Cabalistic Sephiroth. (Janet Farrar and Stewart Farrar, The Life and Times of a Modern Witch [Custer, WA: Phoenix Publishing Company, 1988], 121)

As our study progresses, we will see that these witches were extremely correct with those statements. Dr. William Robert Woodman, an eminent Freemason, was also one of the original founders that worked very hard to establish the Golden Dawn. He was a member of the Ros. Anglia, a Hebrew scholar, and student of the Cabala and also wrote many occult manuscripts.

Dr. William Wynn Westcott

William Wynn Westcott was a London coroner who was forced to choose between his job and the Golden Dawn when the public became aware of his occult activities. Westcott chose to resign as head of the Golden Dawn (at least visibly). Westcott translated the *Sepher Yetzirah*, a Cabalistic text and also wrote a book titled *The Magical Mason*. This Golden Dawn founder belonged to a truly impressive list of occult organizations, which gives us an idea of how these occult organizations network.

Westcott, an English Mason, appointed Junior Grand Deacon to the Grand Lodge of England in 1902 and the head of the Societas Rosicruciana in Anglia and Golden Dawn, was also the secretary of the Rite of Swedenborg, Knight Kadosch in Ancient and Accepted Scottish Rites, Grand Standard Bearer, Royal Arch, Grand Lodge of England, and Regent of the Illuminati and was on intimate terms with one of its founders, the German Theodore Reuss Thirty-third, Ninetieth, Ninety-sixth Degrees.[24]

Westcott also worked closely with Theodor Reuss, the head of the O.T.O. Since their early existence, the O.T.O. and the Golden Dawn have maintained close ties. The father of modern Satanism, Aleister Crowley, was a member of both organizations.

S.L. MacGregor Mathers

The last of the original founders of the Golden Dawn that we will be discussing is S.L. MacGregor Mathers, who was heralded at the turn of the last century as the most powerful and gifted occult practitioner in the world. Mathers was initiated into Freemasonry on 4 October 1877 and became a Master Mason on 30 January 1878.

Mathers took Aleister Crowley and taught him what he needed to know to go on to become the father of modern Satanism. All did not remain peaceful between Mathers and Crowley, and, as the rivalry increased, they actually engaged in a war of black magic. Mathers would receive instructions from "Secret Chiefs" whom Mathers claimed were human beings with superhuman powers.

Mathers wrote what was called *Mathers Manifesto*, a pledge of blind obedience to these "Secret Chiefs." The manifesto stated, "It was requisite that such a member should be one who, while having the necessary and peculiar educational basis of critical and profound occult archaeological knowledge, should at the same time be not only ready but willing to devote himself in every sense to a blind and unreasoning obedience to those Secret Chiefs."[25] Mathers continues, saying,

> he must further pledge himself to obey in everything the commands of the aforesaid Secret Chief's "perinde ac cadaver," body and soul, without question and without argument whether their commands related to magical action in the external world, or to psychic world, military action in the external world, or to psychic action in other worlds and planes, whether Angelic, spiritual or demonic. (Israel Regardie, *What You Should Know about the Golden Dawn* [Phoenix, AZ: Falcon Press, 1987], 181)

Mathers still influences the occult world today through his writings. Mathers wrote one of the classic books on the Kabbalah called *Kabbalah Unveiled*. Mathers also translated two of the most influential books of magical spells,

The Key of Solomon The King, and *The Book of the Sacred Magic of Abramelin, The Maji.*

While Crowley was working the rituals of the *Book of Abramelin,* he became possessed with his lifelong spirit guide (demon), Aiwass. The demon Aiwass dictated, the truly Satanic book *The Book of Law* to Crowley. We have previously studied some parts of that book in the information on the O.T.O.

Arthur Edward Waite

Another man who was initiated into the Golden Dawn at Mathers' home was Arthur Edward Waite. Waite proceeded to become a major force, not only in the occult world, but also in Freemasonry. Waite was praised by one of the greatest Masonic authorities of all time in one of the most popular Masonic books ever written, *The Builders* by Joseph Fort Newton. Newton wrote this tribute to A.E. Waite in *The Builders*: "Perhaps the greatest student in this field of esoteric teaching and method, certainly the greatest now living, is Arthur Edward Waite, to whom it is a pleasure to pay tribute."[26]

Waite was more than a Freemason; he was an authority on Freemasonry and was the author of *A New Encyclopedia of Freemasonry.* Waite is also the author of such occult titles as *The Book of Black Magic* and *Devil Worship in France. The Book of Black Magic* by Waite contains terrible conjurations given in the name of Satan and has spells to conjure Lucifer.

Another of Waite's books is called *The Holy Kabbalah,* which states in its introduction, "For the Kabbalist the ultimate sacrament is the sexual act, carefully organized and sustained as the most perfect mystical trance."[27]

Perhaps, you are beginning to realize the connections between the Golden Dawn and Freemasonry are many. The Golden Dawn was not only founded by Freemasons, but we can also document that in the early stages of the Golden Dawn it had a helping hand from the lodge. The fact can be established that the original Golden Dawn was allowed to use the Mark Masons' Hall to conduct rituals. They were given assistance by Masonic officials, but the lodge was careful that this knowledge didn't become public.

> From the beginning, the ceremonies of Isis-Urania were conducted at Mark Masons' Hall in the Great Queen Street (now demolished), but members were careful not to embarrass the Masonic authorities, being told that they "must not enter Mark Masons' Hall" by the front door, but go under archway and down passage, entering by a door on the right.[28]

One of the early members of the Golden Dawn, Maud Gonne MacBride, left the organization after finding out about the Masonic connections of the order. "Usually the G.D. held their ceremonies in the drawing-room of some member of the Order, but on one occasion I was summoned to an initiation ceremony of the Order in the Mark Masons' Hall in Euston Road. It set me thinking. If they met in a Free-Mason Hall, perhaps the G.D. was an esoteric side of Masonry."[29]

The rituals of the Golden Dawn involved ritual magic, and, to be precise, they summoned and conversed with demons! Nothing could be made any clearer than from reading an official account of their rituals by Israel Regardie. "Yet, if there may arise an absolute necessity for working or conversing with a Spirit of evil nature, and that to retain him before thee without tormenting him, thou hast to employ the symbol of the Pentagram reversed."[30]

It is indeed hard to disagree with the conclusion of our witch experts, Janet and Stewart Farrar, when they stated that the biggest influence in the modern occult explosion has been the Freemasons of the Golden Dawn. The foundational works for ritual magic and Satanism are found in the writings of the men involved in the Golden Dawn. Anton Szandor LaVey, high priest of the Church of Satan gives credit to the Golden Dawn as the source of his satanic invocations found in the Satanic Bible. LaVey tells about his translations: "I have presented my translation of the following calls with an archaic but Satanically correct unvarnishing of the translation employed by the

Order of the Golden Dawn in the late Nineteenth Century. . . . The Enochian Calls are the Satanic paeans of faith."[31]

What about the Farrars' own special field of expertise witchcraft? By now, you can probably guess the answer. They definitely give credit to Freemasonry as one of the sources for the rituals of witchcraft. Doreen Valiente, in particular, contributed much to the final version of Gardner's *Book of Shadows*, the unpublished body of rituals and craft lore traditionally copied out by hand by every new witch from his or her initiator's version.

There is no doubt that the New Forest coven's inherited rituals were fragmentary, and Gardner had set about making them into a workable whole by filling the gaps with material he regarded as suitable from other sources, such as Freemasonry, the writings of Aleister Crowley, and the odd Kipling poem.[32]

Witchcraft and Freemasonry

Many researchers of the occult have pointed out the similarities between the initiation ritual in witchcraft and the Masonic initiation ritual. There are many other similarities between the two crafts that could be documented and compared. One reason for these similarities is the fact that both evolved from an obvious common source, the ancient mystery religions. Another reason is the fact that some of the most powerful and influential witches of modern times have been Freemasons.

Gerald Gardner and Alex Sanders

According to the writings of a Shamani witch, Gwyn Gwynallen, even the very name Wicca, the name often given to modern witchcraft, originated from the writings of the two Freemasonic witches Gerald Gardner and Alex Sanders.

Gardner was a Freemason and also a Lodge Master of the O.T.O. He enlisted help from his fellow O.T.O. member Aleister Crowley in the writing of his rituals. Gardner was known as a sado-masochist and the Gardenian School of Witchcraft is named after him. When Gardner revealed his involvement with witch cults in his 1954 publication, *Witchcraft Today*, he received a torrent of letters, and, within a few years, covens were in operation all over England.

Alex Sanders was a Freemason and a black magician and is also known as the founder of the Alexandrian School of Witchcraft, which is noted for its use of sexual intercourse in the initiation rituals. These two branches of witchcraft or paganism (Gardenian and Alexandrian), to our minds, are Wiccan.[33]

Alex Sanders said he was initiated as a witch when he was seven years old by his grandmother who was a witch. She had him stand nude in a circle with his head down. She took a sharp razor, cut his scrotum to make it bleed slightly, and declared him a witch—a third degree and a black magickian.[34]

Eliphas Levi

Any survey of the history of the relationship between Freemasonry and other occult orders would be incomplete without making mention of the master Freemason, occultist Eliphas Levi. Professor Carl Raschke of the University of Denver does an excellent job of expressing the importance of Eliphas Levi to the occult explosion.

Nearly a century before Crowley, around the middle of the nineteenth century, there rose to fame in France a renegade Catholic rector called Alphonse Constant, who changed his name to Eliphas Levi. Levi was considered the Michelangelo of the suppressed traditions of black magic in the Christian West.[35]

The French occultist Alphonse-Louis Constant (a.k.a. Eliphas Levi), who influenced twentieth-century Satanism considerably, bought almost completely into the thesis that Templars were diabolists. And, his engraving of the Templar idol Baphomet has become a classic article of iconography for today's black magicians, a sort of Satanist Mona Lisa.[36]

Here is an artist's rendition of Levi's engraving of the Baphomet, which was called the "Satanist Mona Lisa" by professor Raschke. [37]

Drawing by Sue Ellen (Glaubman) Ebertz of Levi's
Baphomet

The Satanic Bible by Anton LaVey explains how important this picture is to Satanists:

> The symbol of Baphomet was used by the Knights
> Templar to represent Satan. Through the ages this
> symbol has been called by many different names.
> Among these are: The Goat of Mendes, The Goat
> of a Thousand Young. The Black goat, The Judas
> Goat, and perhaps most appropriately, The Scape-
> goat. Baphomet represents the Powers of Dark-

ness combined with the generative fertility of the goat. . . . The symbol of Baphomet is placed on the wall above the altar. (Anton Szandor LaVey, *The Satanic Bible* [New York, NY: Avon Books, 1969], 136.)

The occult researcher Michael Howard comments on the symbolism of Levi's pantheistic idol, Baphomet, in his book, *The Occult Conspiracy*.

In Levi's illustration, Baphomet is a goat-headed figure with androgynous features who sits on a cube. A torch blazes between the goat's horns which represents cosmic intelligence and spiritual illumination. In occult tradition, Lucifer, who is regarded by the Church as the devil is called the light-bringer because he grants his disciples spiritual illumination through incarnation on the physical plane. (Michael Howard, *The Occult Conspiracy, Secret Societies: Their Influence and Power in Word History* [Rochester, Vermont: Destiny Books, 1989], 38.)

Albert Pike and Eliphas Levi

Eliphas Levi became a Freemason on 14 March 1861 and authored many books that have become classics in occult literature. Many more things than we have already shared could be said about Eliphas Levi, but the information we are dwelling on here is the Luciferian doctrine that Levi passed on to another Freemason of great repute, Albert Pike.

Pike was the Grand Commander of the Scottish Rite from 1859 to 1891 and is called by many the most powerful and influential American Mason of all time. His book *Morals and Dogma*, which was published by the Supreme Council, is still a Masonic classic of great impact. Levi thought of Lucifer not as a person, but as a force; the pantheistic god of the New Age movement, the great magical agent that could be used for good or evil. He explains: "They have said that the Great Magical Agent—accurately termed Lucifer because it is the vehicle of light and the receptacle of all forms is a mediating force diffused throughout creation"[38]

In the Luciferian doctrine of Eliphas Levi, Satan and Lucifer were not evil in the craft sense, they were just another side of Levi's pantheistic god. "Thus Satan is not the ruler of the realm of shadow, he is the agent of light behind a veil. He is of service to God, he performs God's work: God has not rejected him, for he holds him still in his hand. . . . What is the Devil, then, in the final analysis? The Devil is God working evil."[39]

This is the god of *Star Wars*, not a personal god, but just a force that can be used for good like Luke Skywalker or can also be used for evil, like Darth Vader. Albert Pike teaches the same Luciferian doctrine in what is probably the most widely used and honored Masonic book of all time, *Morals and Dogma*.

> The true name of Satan, the Kabalists say, is that of Yahveh reversed; for Satan is not a black god, but the negation of God. The Devil is the personification of Atheism or Idolatry. For the Initiates, this is not a Person, but a Force, created for good, but which may serve for evil. It is the instrument of Liberty or Free Will. They represent this Force, which presides over the physical generation, under the mythologic and horned form of the God Pan; thence came the he-goat of the Sabbat, brother of the Ancient Serpent, and the Light-bearer or Phosphor, of which the poets have made the false Lucifer of the legend. (Albert Pike, *Morals and Dogma* [Richmond, VA: L.H. Jenkins Inc., 1871], 102.)

Most Freemasons don't know that the passage above is a direct quote from page 161 of *The History of Magic*, by the master occultist Eliphas Levi. Albert Pike speaks once again about Lucifer the light-bearer in *Morals and Dogma*. "Lucifer, the Light-bearer! Strange and mysterious name to give to the Spirit of Darkness! Lucifer, the Son of the Morning! Is it he who bears the Light, and with its splendors intolerable blinds feeble, sensual, or selfish Souls? Doubt it not!"[40]

Once again, few Freemasons realize that Albert Pike is quoting directly from page thirty-six of *The History of Magic* by Eliphas Levi. The fact that Albert Pike takes his Luciferian doctrine directly from the occultist Freemason Eliphas Levi can be proven beyond a shadow of a doubt.

Another one of Eliphas Levi's occult drawings is called "the great symbol of Solomon." This drawing also portrayed the false idea that God has an evil side to him as well as a good side. It was explained as "the great Symbol of Solomon. The Double Triangle of Solomon, represented by the two Ancients of the Kabalah; the Macroprosopus and the Microprosopus; the God of Light and the God of Reflections; of mercy and vengeance; the white Jehovah and the black Jehovah."[41]

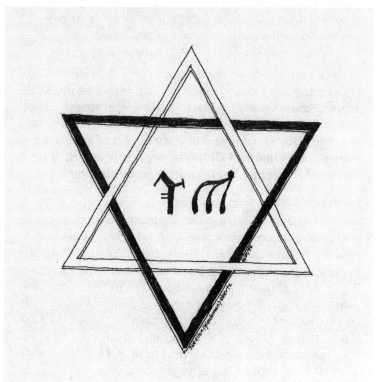

Drawing by Sue Ellen (Glaubman) Ebertz of the Great Symbol of Solomon [42]

The same drawing also appears on page 253 in a recent book called *A Bridge to Light*, published by the Supreme Council, Thirty-third Degree Ancient and Accepted Scottish Rite of Freemasonry Southern Jurisdiction. Speaking of the snake's true identity, the book states that "it is the body of the Holy Spirit, the universal Agent, the Serpent devouring his own tail."[43]

What a blasphemy! What arrogance! Jesus said,

> Wherefore I say unto you, All manner of sin and blasphemy shall be forgiven unto men: but the blasphemy against the Holy Ghost shall not be forgiven unto men. And whosoever speaketh a word against the Son of man, it shall be forgiven him: but whosoever speaketh against the Holy Ghost, it shall not be forgiven him, neither in this world, neither in the world to come. (Matt. 12:31–32)

We have read the explanation from *A Bridge to Light* concerning the snake around Levi's drawing of the white Jehovah and the black Jehovah and the fact that the book claims the snake represents the Holy Spirit. We have told how the book is published by the Supreme Council. How can any man that is a Christian support the distribution of such blasphemy? Such an idea is unthinkable!

Summary

Freemasonry is truly an organization that deceives good men. Many honorable men who are in the lodge actually believe that they belong to a Christian fraternal organization, and nothing could be further from the truth. As we have shown, all Freemasons are in the occult and down through the years, time after time, Masons have come together to organize other occult groups. There is most assuredly more to Freemasonry than most Freemasons realize. Thirty-third Degree Manly P. Hall, Masonry's greatest philosopher, gives us a true picture of Freemasonry:

> Freemasonry is a fraternity within a fraternity, an outer organization concealing an inner brother-

hood of the elect. . . . The visible society is a
splendid camaraderie of free and accepted men
enjoined to devote themselves to ethical, educational, fraternal, patriotic, and humanitarian concerns. The invisible society is a secret and most
august fraternity whose members are dedicated to
the service of a mysterious arcanum
arcanorum. . . . In each generation only a few are
accepted into the inner sanctuary of the work, but
these are veritable princes of truth, and their
sainted names shall be remembered in future age
together with the seers and prophets of the elder
world. . . . They are dwellers upon the threshold
of the innermost, masters of that secret doctrine
which forms the invisible foundation of every great
theological and rational institution. (Manly P. Hall,
Lectures on Ancient Philosophy [Los Angeles, CA:
Philosophical Research Society, Inc., 1984], 433.)

We have presented in a few brief pages a general
review of the relationship between Freemasonry and the
dark side of the occult world. We have documented the
connections between Freemasons and the Illuminati, the
New Age movement, the Theosophical Society, Satanism,
the O.T.O., the Rosicrucian Society, the Golden Dawn,
witchcraft, the Egyptian mystery religions, many history-
making key people, and many famous Freemasons who
were involved with these groups. Much more could have
been said on this subject, but we believe what has been
presented is sufficient enough to show the fact that Freemasons have played the leading roles in the twentieth
century occult explosion.

This is a side of the lodge that Masons don't like to
talk about. However, it is a side that exists nonetheless.
The Scripture admonishes us not to be unequally yoked
with unbelievers, and, when a man can bow his knee at
the Masonic altar and make the Freemasons that we have
discussed in this chapter their lodge brothers, they have
taken upon themselves the most unequal yoke that could
ever be imagined.

Be ye not unequally yoked together with unbelievers: for what fellowship hath righteousness with

unrighteousness? and what communion hath light
with darkness? And what concord hath Christ with
Belial? or what path he that believeth with an in-
fidel? And What agreement hath the temple of
God with idols? for ye are the temple of the living
God; as God hath said, I will dwell in them, and
walk in them; and I will be their God, and they
shall be my people. Wherefore come out from
among them, and be ye separate, saith the Lord,
and touch not the unclean thing; and I will receive
you. And will be a Father unto you, and ye shall
be my sons and daughters, saith the Lord Almighty.
(2 Cor. 6:14–8)

Endnotes

1. *Webster's New International Dictionary*, 3d ed., s.v. "occult."

2. George H. Steinmetz, *The Royal Arch Its Hidden Meaning* (Richmond, VA: Macoy Publishing, 1946), 147.

3. Anton Szandor LaVey, *The Satanic Rituals* (New York, NY: Avon Books, 1972), 78.

4. John Robinson, *Proofs of a Conspiracy* (Western Islands: The Americanist Classics, 1798), 60.

5. Lynn F. Perkins, *New Age Youth and Masonry* (Lakemont, Georgia: CSA Press, 1972), dedication page.

6. Helena Petrovna Blavatsky, *The Secret Doctrine* (London: The Theosophical Publishing House, 1893), 446.

7. Ibid., 220.

8. Joseph J. Carr, *The Twisted Cross* (Lafayette, LA: Huntington House Inc., 1985), 282.

9. Lady Queenborough, *Occult Theocracy* (Printed in Los Angeles, CA: The Christian Book Club of America, 1933), 533.

10. Jerry Johnston, *The Edge of Evil* (United States: Word Publishing, 1989), 136.

11. Alice A. Bailey, *The Externalisation of the Hierarchy* (New York: Lucis Publishing Company, 1957), 511.

12. Foster Bailey, *Things To Come* (New York: Lucis Publishing Company, 1974), 108.

13. Ibid., 110.

14. Ibid., 122.

15. Ibid., 116.

16. Aleister Crowley, *Ancient Wisdom and Secret Sects* (Alexandria, Virginia: Time-Life Books, 1989), 118.

17. Aleister Crowley, *Satanic Extracts* (Black Lodge Publishing, 1991), 4.

18. Francis King, *The Rites of Modern Occult Magic* (New York, NY: The MacMillan Company, 1970), 119.

19. Hymenaeus ed. *The Equinox* (1990), vol. 3, no. 10: 205.

20. John Symonds and Kenneth Grant, *The Confessions of Aleister Crowley*, 771.

21. Albert G. Mackey, *Mackey's Revised Encyclopedia of Freemasonry* (Chicago, IL: The Masonic History Company, 1946), 130.

22. Ellic Howe, *The Magicians of The Golden Dawn* (Ann Arbor, MI: Samuel Weiser, Inc., 1972), 8.

23. Ibid., 47.

24. Lady Queenborough, *Occult Theocracy*, 298.

25. Israel Regardie, *What You Should Know About The Golden Dawn* (Phoenix, AZ: Falcon Press, 1987), 181.

26. Joseph Fort Newton, *The Builders* (Richmond, VA: Macoy Publishing, 1979), 57.

27. A.E. Waite, *The Holy Kabbalah* (Secaucus, NJ: Citadel Press), ix.

28. R. A. Gilbert, *The Golden Dawn Companion* (Wellingborough, Northhamptonshire: The Aquarian Press, 1886), 31.

29. Ellic Howe, *The Magicians of the Golden Dawn* (York Beach, Maine: Samuel Weiser, Inc., 1972), 70.

30. Israel Regardie, *The Golden Dawn* (St. Paul, MN: Llewellyn Publications, 1990), 280.

31. Anton Szandor LaVey, *The Satanic Bible* (New York, NY: Avon Books, 1969), 155-6.

32. Janet and Stewart Farrar, *The Life and Times of a Modern Witch* (Custer, WA: Phoenix Publishing Company), 23.

33. Larry Kahaner, *Cults That Kill, Probing the Underworld of Occult Crime* (New York, NY: Warner Books, 1988), 98.

34. Ibid., 99.

35. Carl A. Raschke, *Painted Black* (New York, NY: Harper and Row, 1990), 37.

36. Ibid., 91.

37. Eliphas Levi, *Transcendental Magic*, trans. A.E. Waite (York Beach, Maine; Samuel Weiser, Inc., 1896), 159.

38. Eliphas Levi, *The History of Magic* (New York, NY: Samuel Weiser, 1913), 159.

39. Eliphas Levi, *The Book of Splendours, The Inner Mysteries of Qabalism Its relationship to Freemasonry, Numerology & Tarot* (York Beach, Maine: Samuel Weiser, Inc., 1973), 72.

40. Albert Pike, *Morals and Dogma* (Richmond, VA: L. H. Jenkins Inc., 1871), 321.

41. Levi, *Transcendental Magic*, 161.

42. Eliphas Levi, "Illustration of Great Symbol, of Solomon," *Transcendental Magic*, xii.

43. Rex R. Hutchens, *A Bridge To Light* (Anderson, South Carolina: The Supreme Council, Thirty-third Degree Ancient and Accepted Scottish Rite of Freemasonry Southern Jurisdiction United States of America, 1988), 253.

Ten

Southern Baptists and Freemasonry: The Story Goes On—and On

J. Edward Decker

While our Freemasonry conference was in session, the talk was all about the ongoing study and eventual Southern Baptist Convention's denominational vote on Freemasonry. Called to do a fair study by the convention a year earlier, the Home Missions Board appointed Dr. Gary Leazer to head up an unbiased review. It turned into a can of worms for everyone involved.

As things turned out, the report became somewhat tainted when it was discovered that Dr. Gary Leazer, the man in charge of the study, was getting "clandestine" help in its preparation from Masonic friends. A letter surfaced during the study, written by Leazer to one of the Masonic leaders, thanking him for all the help and making several depreciating remarks concerning those who were opposed to the lodge. That letter had Leazer removed from his job as head of the study, but both Leazer and the report continued on at the HMB without correction. The report went to the floor of the convention as prepared by Leazer and his Masonic tutors.

Months after the vote was taken, in favor of the Masonic position, Dr. Leazer's obvious ties to the lodge created a new stir within the denomination when a copy of a speech he had made at a Masonic gathering reached the wrong hands.

In the *Columbus Dispatch*, dated 6 November 1993, Religious News Service writer David Anderson reported,

> Larry Lewis, president of the Home Missions Board, said he requested Leazer's resignation for "Gross insubordination" following publication in October of a speech Leazer gave to a Masonic group.

> Lewis said Leazer's Aug. 8 speech violated an order to "refrain from any and all involvement in the Freemasonry issue." Lewis told Baptist Press, the denomination's official news agency, he had accepted Leazer's resignation Oct. 22.

> "He has clearly violated that directive and in doing so has demonstrated his unwillingness to submit to the authority of his supervisors," Lewis said. Whether Baptists can also be members of a Masonic Lodge has been a volatile issue.

The Convention and the Vote: The Afterglow

It's an amazing thing that after the smoke had all settled, the Freemasons declared a mighty victory at the SBC. In the *Scottish Rite Journal*, the Grand Commander C. Fred Kleinknecht called the vote historic, saying, "this [vote was the] significant turning point for modern Freemasonry."[1]

And, well it might be. The Masonic fraternity believes it has withstood its most severe challenge in more than a century.

To the shame of the SBC's commitment to biblical standards, the convention, by an overwhelming majority, approved the report and recommendation on Freemasonry issued by the SBC Home Missions Board, which listed a number of things about Freemasonry that were compatible with Christianity and a number of things that were not. The report went on to say that membership in a Masonic order was the business of the individual, not the church.

The Masonic Grand Commander called it a great victory. He stated that by its vote, the SBC had "joined Freemasonry in its elevation of individual conscience as the guide to personal beliefs and actions."

In a letter addressed to "All Active Members, Deputies of the Supreme Council, Representatives and Secretaries," dated 21 June 1993, Kleinknecht again inferred that vote was a great victory for the craft. He stated, "The Board's [Home Missions Board] report, based on a nearly year-long study by the SBC's Interfaith Witness Department, rejects the allegation that Freemasonry is incompatible with Christianity and Southern Baptist Doctrine."

It sure sounded like a victory for the craft so far, but he mentioned one problem a little further in his letter. He said, "Although the report contains 8 unjustified, we feel, specific criticisms of Freemasonry, it also includes several commendations of Freemasonry."

Let's back up just a hair. The Leazer affair proved without doubt that the Masons, themselves, were involved with the report and aided the man in charge of writing the report. Even then, they were unable to prevent the mention of some specific criticisms of Freemasonry.

Next, the Masons made an unprecedented push to get control of the convention. The same Grand Commander wrote a letter to all those addressed above, plus the editors of all Masonic publications and said that "It is crucial that Masons who are Southern Baptists become messengers to the Southern Baptist Convention."

On the back of Kleinknecht's letter was a twelve step plan for every Baptist Mason to follow in getting to be a messenger at the SBC. The Masons rallied as never before in their history. Only the Masons know what percentage of the 17,800 Messengers were Masons.

Yet, in spite of the enormous efforts by the Masons, the report still listed a number of things so wrong with

Freemasonry that if they were reviewed in context of biblical Christianity, no Christian could truly be a Mason. This is what they said:

The Eight Problems with Freemasonry

1. The prevalent use of offensive concepts, titles, and terms such as "Worshipful Master" for the leaders of the lodge; references to their buildings as "mosques," "shrines," or "temples"; and the use of such words as "Abaddon" and Jah-Bul-On," the so-called secret name of God. To many, these terms are not only offensive but sacrilegious.

2. The use of archaic, offensive rituals and so-called "bloody oaths" or "obligations," among those being that promised by the Entered Apprentice: [sic] or that of the Fellow Craft degree: [sic] Or that of the Master Mason: [sic] Or that of other advanced degrees with required rituals considered by many to be pagan and incompatible with Christian faith and practice.

Even though these oaths, obligations and rituals may or may not be taken seriously by the initiate, it is inappropriate for a Christian to "sincerely promise and swear," with a hand on the Holy Bible, any such promises or oaths, or to participate in any such pagan rituals.

3. The recommended readings in pursuance of advanced degrees, of religions and philosophies, which are undeniably pagan and/or occult, such as much of the writings of Albert Pike, Albert Mackey, Manly Hall, Rex Hutchins, W.L. Wilmhurst and other such authors; along with their works, such as Morals and Dogma, A Bridge to Light, An Encyclopedia of Freemasonry and The Meaning of Masonry.

4. The reference to the Bible placed on the altar of the lodge as the "furniture of the lodge," com-

paring it to the square and compass rather than giving it the supreme place in the lodge.

5. The prevalent use of the term "light" which some may understand as a reference to salvation rather than knowledge or truth.

6. The implication that salvation may be attained by one's good works, implicit in the statement found in some Masonic writings that "Masonry is continually reminded of that purity of life and conduct which is necessary to obtain admittance into the Celestial Lodge above where the Supreme Architect of the Universe presides."

Even though many Masons understand that the "purity of life and conduct" can only be achieved through faith in Jesus Christ, others may be led to believe they can earn salvation by living a pure life with good conduct.

7. The heresy of Universalism (the belief all people will eventually be saved), which permeates the writings of many Masonic authors, which is a doctrine inconsistent with New Testament teaching.

8. The refusal of most lodges (although not all) to admit for membership African Americans. (Reported by the Home Missions Board, SBC, 1350 Spring Street NW, Atlanta, GA 30367-5601)

On the positive side, the report commended the Masons for its many charitable endeavors, hospitals, burn centers. It acknowledged that many outstanding Christians and Southern Baptists now and in the past have been Masons.

They recognized that many of the tenets and teachings of some Grand Lodges could be considered compatible and supportive of the Christian faith and practice, such as a strong emphasis on honesty, integrity, industry, and character and the insistence that every member believe in a god. The report then quoted a number of biblical quotes from the Texas monitor to show that there are some explicit references to the Christian faith.

However, the report cautioned that "To be sure, not all Grand Lodges affirm Christian Doctrine, and many do not declare Jesus as the unique Son of God; but many do, and for this we commend them."

Their final statement concludes,

"We exhort Southern Baptists to prayerfully and carefully evaluate Freemasonry in the light of the Lordship of Christ, the teachings of the Scripture, and the findings of this report, as led by the Holy Spirit of God." And we say that if a Christian Mason truly did that he would honestly have to leave the lodge.

Dr. James Holly is the president of Mission and Ministry to Men, 550 N. 10th Street, Beaumont, TX, 77702. He has been God's man of the hour for the Southern Baptists. He has taken a strong stand time and again both as an official messenger to the convention and as an individual member of the denomination. He has almost single-handedly brought this issue to the place where Freemasonry is being exposed as the terrible threat it truly is to the church.

Dr. Holly has been cursed, slandered, and defamed for his efforts but continues to demand that the HMB admit that the report was slanted and that the convention vote was skewed in favor of the many Baptist Masons. He has continued to ask the SBC leaders to reevaluate their stand. In a recent letter to the Home Mission Executive Committee, dated 9 February 1994, he responded to a HMB resolution justifying their SBC report:

> The Executive Committee's affirmation of its own actions is disingenuous. It was Dr. Lewis himself who said that the HMB was in a "no win Situation" in regard to the study of Freemasonry. It was Dr. Lewis himself who said that if the HMB found for the Lodge or if they found against the Lodge the HMB would lose money. The Executive Committee's praise of its own work rings hollow in the face of the obvious deficiencies of the HMB's

handling of the study of Freemasonry. . . . the HMB's *A Study of Freemasonry* is not objective, scholarly or thorough.

Until the Southern Baptists take on this issue from a biblical position and not a political one, the denomination will wallow in self-destructive cover-up after cover-up. Pray that the Holy Spirit of God will break through the darkness in high places and set the SBC free.

Endnotes

1. C. Fred Kleinknecht, Scottish Rite Journal (August 1993): 3–6.

ORDER THESE HUNTINGTON HOUSE BOOKS !

_____ America: Awaiting the Verdict—Mike Fuselier	4.99	_____
_____ America Betrayed—Marlin Maddoux	6.99	_____
_____ Beyond Political Correctness—David Thibodaux	9.99	_____
_____ A Call to Manhood—David E. Long	9.99	_____
_____ Conservative, American & Jewish—Jacob Neusner	9.99	_____
_____ The Dark Side of Freemasonry—Ed Decker	9.99	_____
_____ Deadly Deception: Freemasonry—Tom McKenney	8.99	_____
_____ Don't Touch That Dial—Barbara Hattemer & Robert Showers	9.99/19.99	_____
_____ En Route to Global Occupation—Gary Kah	9.99	_____
_____ *Exposing the AIDS Scandal—Dr. Paul Cameron	7.99/2.99	_____
_____ The Extermination of Christianity—Paul Schenck	9.99	_____
_____ Freud's War with God—Jack Wright, Jr.	7.99	_____
_____ Goddess Earth—Samantha Smith	9.99	_____
_____ Gays & Guns—John Eidsmoe	7.99/14.99	_____
_____ Heresy Hunters—Jim Spencer	8.99	_____
_____ Hidden Dangers of the Rainbow—Constance Cumbey	9.99	_____
_____ Hitler and the New Age—Bob Rosio	9.99	_____
_____ Homeless in America—Jeremy Reynalds	9.99	_____
_____ How to Homeschool (Yes, You!)—Julia Toto	4.99	_____
_____ *Inside the New Age Nightmare—Randall Baer	9.99/2.99	_____
_____ A Jewish Conservative Looks at Pagan America—Don Feder	9.99/19.99	_____
_____ Kinsey, Sex and Fraud—Dr. Judith A. Reisman & Edward Eichel (Hard cover)	11.99	_____
_____ The Liberal Contradiction—Dale A. Berryhill	7.99	_____
_____ Legalized Gambling—John Eidsmoe	9.99	_____
_____ Loyal Opposition—John Eidsmoe	8.99	_____
_____ The Media Hates Conservatives—Dale A. Berryhill	9.99	_____
_____ Out of Control—Brenda Scott	9.99	_____
_____ Please Tell Me—Tom McKenney	9.99	_____
_____ Political Correctness—David Thibodaux	9.99	_____
_____ Prescription Death—Dr. Reed Bell & Frank York	9.99	_____
_____ *The Question of Freemasonry—Ed Decker	2.99	_____
_____ Real Men—Dr. Harold Voth	9.99	_____
_____ "Soft Porn" Plays Hardball—Dr. Judith A. Reisman	8.99/16.99	_____
_____ Subtle Serpent—Darylann Whitemarsh & Bill Reisman	9.99	_____
_____ Teens and Devil Worship—Charles Evans	8.99	_____
_____ *To Moroni With Love—Ed Decker	2.99	_____
_____ Trojan Horse—Brenda Scott & Samantha Smith	9.99	_____
_____ When the Wicked Seize a City—Chuck & Donna McIlhenny with Frank York	9.99	_____

*Available in Salt Series

Shipping & Handling _____

TOTAL _____

AVAILABLE AT BOOKSTORES EVERYWHERE or order direct from:
Huntington House Publishers•P.O. Box 53788•Lafayette, LA 70505
Send check/money order. For faster service use VISA/MASTERCARD
Call toll-free 1-800-749-4009.
Add: Freight and handling, $3.50 for the first book ordered, and $.50 for
each additional book up to 5 books.

Enclosed is $_____including postage.
VISA/MASTERCARD #_____ Exp. Date _____
Name_____ Phone: (   )_____
Address_____
City, State, Zip_____